Magic Show

Magic Show

Jonathan Allen & Sally O'Reilly

With contributions by Simon During, Brigitte Felderer, Peter Lamont, Pierre Taillefer, Helen Varola and Marina Warner

SOUTHBANK CENTRE HAYWARD PUBLISHING

Published on the occasion of *Magic Show*

A Hayward Touring exhibition organised
in collaboration with QUAD, Derby

Exhibition tour:
QUAD, Derby
28 November 2009 – 31 January 2010
Grundy Art Gallery, Blackpool
13 February – 10 April 2010
Tullie House Museum and Art Gallery, Carlisle
15 May – 4 July 2010
Chapter, Cardiff
30 July – 12 September 2010
Pump House Gallery, Battersea, London
6 October – 19 December 2010

Curated by Jonathan Allen and Sally O'Reilly

Organised by Isobel Harbison with Rahila Haque
and Sophie Brown

Art Publisher: Mary Richards
Publishing Co-ordinator: Amy Botfield
Sales Manager: Deborah Power

Catalogue designed by Susanna Edwards
and Joseph Harries
www.susannaedwards.com
www.josephharries.com

Printed in Belgium by Die Keure

Published by Hayward Publishing
Southbank Centre
Belvedere Road
London SE1 8XX
www.southbankcentre.co.uk

Translators: Helen Slater (p. 28) and
Malcolm Phillips and Amy Botfield (pp. 108-9)

ISBN 978 1 85332 281 5

A catalogue record for this book is available from the
British Library.

Distributed in the United Kingdom, Europe and
Australasia by Cornerhouse Publications,
70 Oxford Street, Manchester M1 5NH
T +44 (0)161 200 1503
F +44 (0)161 200 1504
www.cornerhouse.org/books

Distributed in North, Central and South America by
D.A.P./Distributed Art Publishers,
155 Sixth Avenue, 2nd Floor, New York, NY 10013
T +212 627 1999
F +212 627 9484
www.artbook.com

Cover: Colin Guillemet, *Untitled (anything but a rabbit)*,
2006 (detail)

HAYWARD TOURING
SOUTHBANK
CENTRE

ARTS COUNCIL ENGLAND
Supported by
ARTS COUNCIL
ENGLAND

Contents

Foreword

THE history of art is riddled with perceptual and conceptual games of trickery and subterfuge. Even pictorial perspective is a system of illusion. The demand for truth, whether to materials or an idea, cannot be sustained, because art is essentially grounded in untruth, the fabrication of alternative versions of reality. As a result, many contemporary artists are as fascinated as their predecessors with the theatrical conventions of magic and conjuring, often deploying the devices of the stage performer to subvert habitual assumptions of cause and effect. Vanishing acts, inexplicable transformations and displays of extraordinary psychic prowess are staples of the stage magician, and the artist may play with these same forms of manipulation and mystification, not for entertainment but to reveal something about the fundamental relationship between matter and the mind. How far can the wish for change overcome the inertia of the material world, which so often defeats us and resists our interventions?

That this is a political as well as poetic or metaphysical question is one of the implicit themes of *Magic Show*. Dictators famously tend to be obsessed with supernaturalism and occult powers, and conjuring metaphors pervade popular political debate in our own society. In contrast to the politician's sometimes deceitful and nefarious ends, however, the artist's use of magic is generally constructive, even if through apparently disruptive means. If the world is changed, it is only for an instant or in a limited location – although awareness of the possibility may have long-lasting effects on the viewer's perception. Irony and self-deflation permeate much of the work in *Magic Show*, undermining claims to authenticity with a clear hint that what appears to be is not necessarily so; the illusion produced is in the mind of the spectator. True and false belief are confounded when the artist declares that it does not actually matter whether or not magical powers supposedly invested in an object really exist; the viewer's mental projection is the more interesting phenomenon. If this implies anthropological detachment, however, that is only a part of the picture; for many of these artists the ideas, imagery and atmosphere of the magician's act are themselves a source of primitive delight. We are connected through our credulity with our childhood selves.

Magic Show was conceived by Jonathan Allen and curated with the writer on art and the history of ideas, Sally O'Reilly. As an artist, writer and long-term researcher on magic (he is an associate curator of The Magic Circle Museum, London) Allen is uniquely qualified to navigate between the worlds of contemporary art and theatrical magic, and his intimate acquaintance with the techniques, histories and theories of the subject is inscribed in every aspect of this project. O'Reilly's acutely critical understanding of contemporary art, combined with a playfully irreverent attitude to cultural hierarchies, has provided a perfect complement to Allen's specialist knowledge and recognition of magic's somewhat marginalised status. The result is a book and exhibition brimming with stimulating ideas, intriguing imagery and arcane allusions. It should be stressed that the focus here is on what cultural historian Simon During has termed 'secular' magic, that is, magic that does not claim supernatural agency or religious belief. Conjuring tricks and sleights of hand may seem far removed from religious cults of miraculous transformation and healing, yet the two are historically linked, sometimes in opposition – as the church's persecution of witchcraft and sorcery illustrates.

The distinction between confidence trickster and saint or shaman has traditionally depended on the examination and ruling of an official adjudicator, whether church, police or committee of elders – or, if these concepts are transferred to the world of art, to critics and museum and gallery curators. (Hence the confusion and frustration of the uninitiated when informed solemnly by figures of authority that an object which, to their eyes, seems to be almost nothing is in fact a significant and valuable work of art.) The notion of magical transfiguration lies at the heart of artistic creation and criticism, whether the values espoused are secular or otherwise.

This immensely fertile terrain is open to many different interpretations. The choice of artists in *Magic Show* reflects the curators' particular concern with the performative, with theatrical enactment or the implication of instrumental power in the artistic gesture or poetic object. This emphasis is reinforced in the archival section of the book and exhibition, which discloses some of the props, paraphernalia and imagery associated with the stage magician, little seen material from collections whose wealth can only be hinted at in this small selection. The archive has a crucial place here, firstly because Allen's knowledge and expertise offer a rare opportunity to consider the two normally separate realms of art and magic within the same frame; secondly, because its themes of politics and conflict, belief and popular religion, commerce and advertising resonate through the exhibition.

In their introductory essays, the curators discuss magic from the points of view of the contemporary artist and the cultural theorist and historian. O'Reilly considers the trope of the magician as a confounder of commonly understood laws of empirical reality and a source of bewilderment and wonder, in contrast to contemporary art's often-perceived role as a liberating tool of demystification and transgression. Allen reflects on the growth of interest in theatrical magic among historians and cultural theorists and the evolving dialogue with magic's own academy, with reference to key critical texts. In his discussion of the magician as a protean figure operating at the boundaries of epistemology, Allen's and O'Reilly's concerns meet, in the recognition that both magicians and artists may pass over metaphysical power for its metafictional counterpart.

In addition to these two essays, this publication includes six short commissioned texts by writers who have made important contributions to the study and history of magic and illusion from a variety of perspectives and disciplines, including psychology, etymology and literary and cultural studies. They have each responded to the curators' invitation to illuminate a single aspect or image, with brilliant concision. In the foldout section the landscape broadens further, as the reader is guided through a century or more of visual and written material on the exhibition's central themes. An appendix contains extracts from André Breton's *L'Art Magique*, translated into English here for the first time. The curators have jointly written the commentaries in the artists' section, which bring all 24 artists into focus from this very particular perspective.

Magic Show expands upon issues that have been debated in several exhibitions and publications over the past decade. One point of departure is the exhibition *Con Art* at Site Gallery, Sheffield (2002), which grew out of a chance meeting at a magic show in New York between Allen and the curators Helen and P.G. Varola, and a subsequent collaboration with Carol Maund. Other related exhibitions include the Hayward Gallery's *Eyes, Lies and Illusions* (2004), *Variety* at the De La Warr Pavilion, Bexhill-on-Sea (2005), *Strange Powers* at Creative Time in New York (2006), *The Great Transformation* at the Frankfurter Kunstverein (2008) and *Zauberkünste* at the Nordico Museum in Linz (2009), curated by Brigitte Felderer (who has contributed, like Helen Varola, to this publication). In 2007 Allen was invited to guest-edit an edition of the New York-based quarterly *Cabinet* on magic, for which he commissioned a text by Ian Saville and O'Reilly, whose interest in esotericism and interdisciplinary performance histories make her a natural collaborator for this project.

We thank the curators for the extraordinary energy, imagination and absolute commitment with which they have approached every aspect of this exhibition and publication. The artists have all responded generously to our invitation to participate, and we are privileged to be able to include so many outstanding works from a wide variety of sources. We are grateful also to the lenders who have allowed us to borrow for a relatively lengthy tour. The exhibition will take a markedly different form at each of its venues, with special programmes of performances and events occurring throughout the tour. *Magic Show* owes a debt of gratitude to many individuals within the theatrical magic community in Britain and abroad. For generous loans to the catalogue and archive section of the exhibition, particular thanks are due to The Magic Circle in London, and to its museum, archive and library staff, headed respectively by Lionel Russell and Tim Reed, David Hibberd and Peter Lane. The Magic Circle's Vice-President, Scott Penrose, has been an invaluable source of creative and logistical support, as has Honorary Vice-President and magic historian Eddie Dawes, both of whom have also made substantial contributions to the *Magic Show* archive. Stage effects designer and magic historian Paul Kieve must be thanked for the loan of, and commentaries on, five extraordinary magic posters for the exhibition tour and for the additional loan of an extensive selection from his collection for the showing at QUAD.

Magic Show was organised in collaboration with QUAD Derby, and our colleagues Louise Clements and Alfredo Cramerotti have played an extremely active role in its development, engaging wholeheartedly with the ideas and the practical challenges, helping with the production of works and supplementing the core exhibition with a special display from Paul Kieve's collection. We have also worked closely with the Grundy Art Gallery in Blackpool, whose curator Stuart Tulloch has supported the project with enormous enthusiasm and been instrumental in obtaining funding for a major new commission by the artist Sinta Werner. We are immensely grateful to the Henry Moore Foundation and the Goethe Institute in London – and specifically to Maja Grafe, the Institute's Project Coordinator for the Visual Arts and Music – for providing financial support for Werner, who will install her work, especially conceived for each space, at most venues on the tour. In Blackpool the exhibition coincides with the annual Blackpool Magic Convention, the largest event of its kind in the world, thus providing a direct link between the fields of contemporary art and professional entertainment. Further new commissions and performance events will accompany the show at Chapter in Cardiff and the Pump House Gallery in Battersea Park, London. We thank colleagues at all *Magic Show* venues, notably Adam Buss, Deputy Director at QUAD, Fiona Venables, Visual Arts Officer at Tullie House, Carlisle, Hannah Firth, curator at Chapter, and Sandra Ross, curator at the Pump House Gallery.

The exhibition has been organised at the Hayward by Isobel Harbison and Rahila Haque, with customary dedication and efficiency, and in the later stages by Sophie Brown, who has taken responsibility for the opening showing. Among colleagues at the Southbank Centre who have contributed, we owe special thanks to Art Publisher Mary Richards and Publishing Co-ordinator Amy Botfield who, with designers Susanna Edwards and Joseph Harries, have produced a book that exceeds our expectations.

Roger Malbert
Senior Curator, Hayward Touring

Acknowledgements

Hayward Touring would like to thank the following individuals and organisations for helping to make the exhibition possible:

Annely Juda Fine Art, London: Jo Spice, Laura Henderson; Francisca Bagulho; Fundació Joan Brossa: Mercè Centellas; Channel 4: Paul McAllister; Dvir Gallery, Tel Aviv: Shir Kochavi; Gagosian Gallery, New York/London: Domenica Stagno, James McKee, Gary Waterston; Greengrassi, London: Megan O'Shea; Galerija Gregor Podnar, Berlin: Marie Graftieaux, Gregor Podnar; Lisson Gallery, London: Silvia Sgualdini, Charlotte Nijssen; Manhattan Loft Corporation: Harry Handelsman, Philippa Cochrane, Melanie Dias; Marian Goodman Gallery, New York: Rose Lord; The Estate of Juan Muñoz: Sandra Feio, Cristina Iglesias; Bruce Nauman Studio: Juliet Myers; Objective Productions: Debi Roach, Anthony Owen; Michael Vine; Timothy Taylor Gallery, London: Ann-Marie James, Saskia Goodway; Vilma Gold, London: Laura Lord, David Thain, Alice Theobald; White Cube, London: Simona Pizzi.

The curators would like to extend their gratitude and respect to all who have offered their support, knowledge, advice and material:

Stan Allen, Mike Austin, Helene Bagger, Jacopo Benci, Gloria Bordons de Porrata-Doria, Helen Brough, Derren Brown, Christine Burgin, Mike Caveney, Mercè Centalles, Jason Cooper, Anne Davenport, Betty Davenport, Edwin A. Dawes, Simon During, Mark Enstone, Jury Everhartz, Simon Faithfull, Brigitte Felderer, Matt Field, John Fisher, Mark Foxwell, Jim Hagy, Aisling Hedgecock, David Hibberds, Volker Huber, Joshua Jay, Bill Kalush, Richard Kaufman, Paul Kieve, Dick Koorwinder, Herbert Lachmayer, Peter Lamont, Peter Lane, Julie Lawson, Bob Loomis, Martin MacMillan, Michael Mangan, Elizabeth McAlpine, Jamie McCarthy, Sina Najafi, Andy Nyman, Anthony Owen, Scott Penrose, Malcolm Phillips, Vanessa Rato, Tim Reed, Julian Rothenstein, Fergus Roy, Allen Ruppersberg, Lionel Russell, Aura Satz, Adrian Searle, Derrick Speight, Jim Steinmeyer, Pierre Taillefer, Stinna Toft, Helen Varola, P.G. Varola, Michael Vine, Marina Warner, Chris Wasshuber, Dan Wolfe, The Conjuring Arts Research Centre, New York, and The Magic Circle, London.

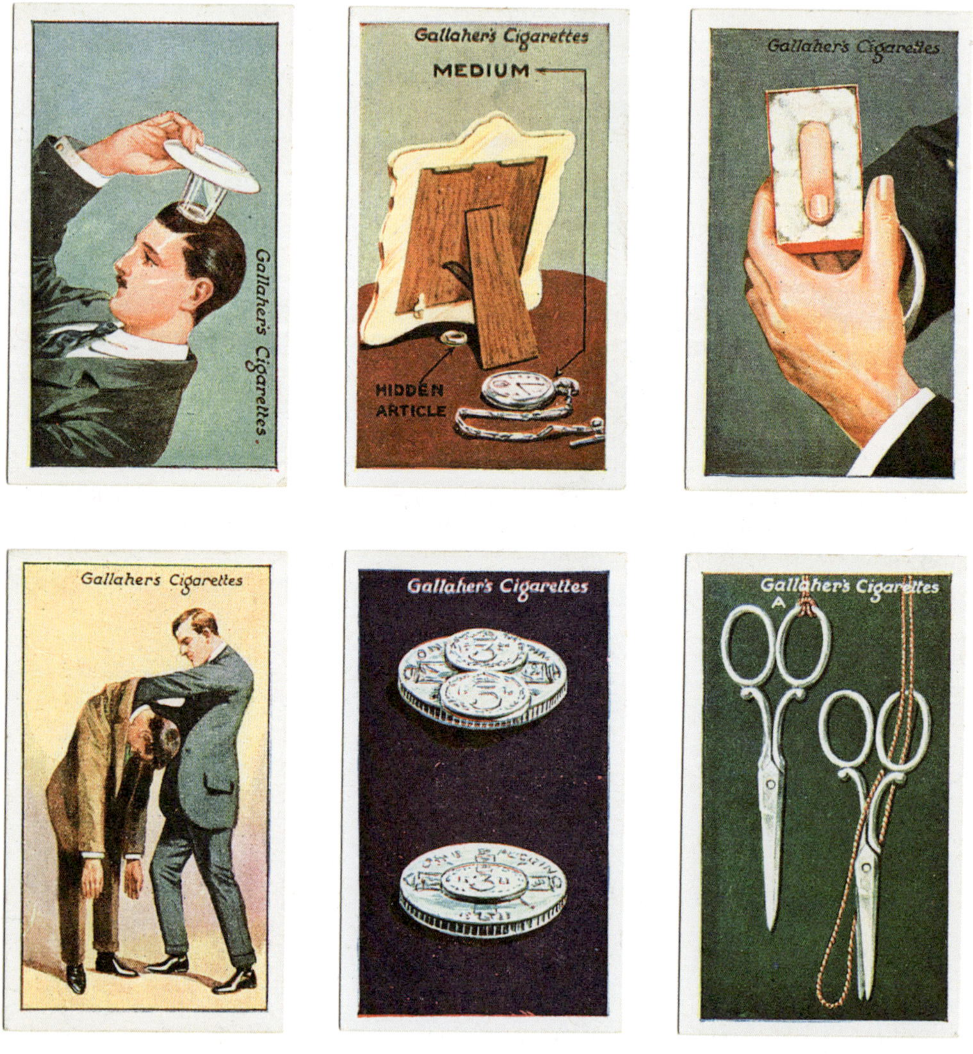

↑ Cigarette cards, Gallaher's Tricks and Puzzles, 1933

Bewildering Logic

SALLY O'REILLY

Bewilderment can be a blunt cudgel, knocking the sensibility from a person and rendering them ineffectual; but it can also be a tickling stick that teases out alternative and contingent modes of thinking in order to deal with lapses in logic. But while there's a vast difference in effect between distressing confusion and delectable mystification, the means are similar. Authoritative control, the double bluff, the red herring, the contrived coincidence and the outright lie are familiar fictional devices that have suffused all aspects of culture and history, from everyday experience to global politics, reflective thought to decisive action. And although we may feel that fact and fiction *should* be distinguishable from one another, on the ground it is nigh impossible to peel them apart.

But then we might ask whether it is vital that these ploys are discernible, or if we perhaps glean more insight into ourselves and our place in the universe when we don't know up from down. The condition of bewilderment arises when the solidity of the narrative we call logic starts to melt away. While the inexplicable has historically been explained by way of supernatural agents of one form or another, it is now eyed more sceptically and, indeed, logically, being variously attributed to anomalous statistical patterning, synchronicity or rogue behaviour. Science, it seems, can explain the inexplicable as something yet to be invited into its fold. It is in this region, however, at the edge of the credible, that artists operate best, reflecting on life, whether experienced or imagined, and wrenching it from the rationalising, ordering tentacles of science. The artist is most likely still an arch-sceptic though, representing the fantastical or ridiculous not to convey esoteric belief, but rather to take delight in confusion and disarray.

But there is another figure that treads this line between reality and fantasy, tugging the strings of our scepticism to slightly different ends. The theatrical magician drums up our rationalising impulses only to divert them towards atavistic credulity, partially and temporarily reviving ancient beliefs in otherworldly powers. Contemporary stage magic has a complex relationship with rational materialism. While it developed from pre-Enlightenment belief structures such as mythology, folkloric superstition and polytheism, magic fractured in the 18th and 19th centuries into spiritualist, occult and theatrical forms, each of which indulged, in very different ways, a continued predisposition towards non-rational impulses. It is the theatrical form that particularly interests us here as it chimes with sceptical art that pivots on illusion and evocation, rather than on faith and immanence. Stage magic does not require audience members to truly believe, but does ask them to hang their scepticism on a peg just outside the auditorium, keeping sharp derision from pricking the bubble of delicious mystification. But where the magician redirects or manipulates credulity to produce temporary, convivial bewilderment in the name of entertainment, the artists in *Magic Show* employ these strategies for the purposes of re-evaluation with varying degrees of gravity, from the gentle prompting of subjective fantasy to political and institutional critique.

If we think of the Enlightenment as the advancement of knowledge by rational means and an attempt to purge the world of chaotic elements, both art and stage magic can be thought of as performing a counter-Enlightenment stance. While both are disruptive of logical positivism and scientific rigour, they do not institute replacement orthodoxies, but instead continue to perform acts of disruption with nauseous inconclusiveness.

In fact, following art's historical legacy – where value was inherent in religious iconography, signification of social status or formalist or utopian credentials – we are left now with a practice that, crudely speaking, is valued (other than by way of its price tag) as an interrogator of orthodoxies. A common demand made of art is that it should square up to complacency, narrow-mindedness and ignorance; create friction against workaday rationalism; elevate the absurd, the useless, the defunct, the irreverent or the perverse, and generally transgress norms. Art is expected to abolish such palatable notions as narrative genre and harmonious closure, and muddy categories that are instrumental to the academy or mainstream entertainment by presenting ambiguities or fragmentation that solicit invention from a viewer wishing to find meaning. Whether or not you condone this pedagogical or ethical remit for art – or indeed believe these demands are ever truly met – is another matter, but the fact remains that an often articulated hope for art is that it should be allowed to move uncompromised and uncompromisingly through, beneath and around the rigid structures of necessity.

This progressive or transcendent view of art might be compared with the perception of magic as the uncanny manipulation of matter usually in thrall to the laws of physics. Theatrical magic makes no claim to supernatural agency, and yet it still carries the vestiges of ancient communing with deities, devils and undisclosed forces and can therefore, by analogy, prompt a re-evaluation of the relationships between perception and reality, transgression and power. Although the stage illusionist benignly enthrals us with these gaps and slippages, confining events to the abstract realm of the auditorium and rarely producing any real or lasting outcome, the potency of such control over human perceptual apparatus is not trivial. The realisation that we have been duped may be, in such cases, harmlessly entertaining, but there are plenty of occasions when the effects of duplicity truly hurt.

The artist might implement these processes to scrutinise mechanisms of power of a different order, making the effect more perilous by relocating it to real-life scenarios or pitching it at a near-ontological intensity. For many artists in *Magic Show*, the contravention of categories and misplacement of ideas or artefacts is a political gesture, echoing the surrealists' eradication of hierarchically inscribed borders between inner and outer worlds, the possible and the improbable. In Joan Brossa's 'object poems' (see p. 53), for instance, lyrical transmutations of archetypal objects seem to refute the Platonic notion that all that is real is possible, but not all that is possible is real. In Franco's Spain this had obvious resonance with revolutionary ideas of radical regime change, but for today's artists the question remains whether such propositional objects alone are a powerful enough catalyst. This is an issue that the Center for Tactical Magic (see p. 58) often broaches through direct action, deploying the magician's tactics within communities to facilitate change through discussion. *The Ultimate Jacket* could lead to thoroughly transgressive behaviour and, although this promise can't be entirely fulfilled by a singular art object, subversive acts can be rehearsed in the mind of each viewer.

Indeed, generally speaking, artists tend to forsake illustrative representation or demonstrative action, opting instead to induce the equivalent thought, experience, sensation or emotion in their audience. An artwork that exemplifies this in *Magic Show* borrows its workings from archaic magic: the empty plinth of Tom Friedman's *Untitled (A Curse), an eleven-inch spherical space eleven inches above a pedestal cursed by a witch* is animated entirely through our reading of the title. This displacement of means – from the authoritative object or image to a more dynamic, audience-oriented form of authorship – is a comparatively recent phenomenon in art. In 1967 Richard Serra began collating *Verb List Compilation: Actions to Relate to Oneself,* which ran like a shopping list of actions for the materially led artist: 'to rotate, to swirl, to support, to hook, to suspend, to spread, to hang, to collect, of tension, of gravity, of entropy, of nature, of grouping, of layering'. The list identifies a practice – and a wider tendency in art of the last century – that deals in brute manipulation of solid matter. These days, however, art seems more aligned with the verbs attributed to theatrical magic, where materiality is made mobile, porous or otherwise fluid: to produce, to vanish, to transpose, to transform, to restore, to penetrate, to levitate, to suspend, of clairvoyancy, of physical anomaly. While this is a shorter list, its implications are wider, as the very nature of substance quivers and its solidity becomes doubtful. Art's current programme of investigation seems to relegate the static and comprehensible to the realm of improbability, instead holding a mirror up to a world that is fractured and ambiguous, where meaning is conditional and up for debate. This appears to echo the counterintuitive developments of 20th-century science – where appearances are volatile as atomic entities seem to communicate, even empathise, across vast distances, changing state or position as the result of observation. And similarly, while stage magicians appeal to an audience who believe their own eyes and an experience of the material world that is distinctly pre-Einsteinian, they make objects appear, disappear and generally behave with disregard for Cartesian niceties such as rational forces and empirical causality.

Ansuman Biswas & Jem Finer bring science and magic directly together in *Zero Genie* (see p. 51), where parabolic flight enables the reconstruction of an ancient archetype. While the work comically exaggerates a parity between the exoticised and the otherworldly, it also reminds us that technology and magic have had a reciprocal relationship throughout history, with inventions and discoveries such as lenses, electricity and film enabling more and more spectacular performances, often of a necromantic or phantasmagorical nature, while, conversely, attempts to communicate with the dead during the First World War gave rise to the technology of early wireless radio.

Zoe Beloff's three-dimensional films of operettas, relating psychotic episodes in real-life psychiatric case studies, bridge spectacularising technology and the internal workings of the human mind through pathology and comic dramatisation. Psychoanalysis, as another major advancement in 20th-century epistemology, has proven invaluable to magicians and artists alike for evaluating, predicting and diverting audience reactions, which, while internalised and subjective, can cause effects that are no less spectacular. We might think of psychoanalysis as a contemporary form of divination, whereby causes are glimpsed, albeit momentarily and without guarantee of their control. But where divination explains what has been and what will come, psychoanalysis identifies current behavioural tropes and mental mechanisms, which artists and magicians can tap into, using archetypes and habits of looking to subvert our expectations, short-circuit logic and apparently perform the incredible.

In his psychoanalytic writings on primitive tribes and magical thinking Sigmund Freud links magic and art through the practice of evocation, where associations or imagery are conjured by means of illusions and perform the accomplishment of desires. Some of the work in *Magic Show* may appear to be of anthropological or shamanistic origin, particularly Brian Catling's mythological props and personae, which divulge neither the nature of their potency nor the desires that guide them (see p. 56), and Alexandra Hopf's *Gehülfen* ('Assistants', see p. 73). Hopf's portraits refer to the tribe of characters that Walter Benjamin identifies as recurring throughout Kafka's stories, which are 'neither members of, nor strangers to, any of the other groups of figures, but, rather, messengers from one to the other'. In Kafka's stories these characters constitute the connective tissue between the protagonist and the unseen world order, activating a situation, carrying out orders or galvanising action. They recall the abiding figure of the trickster, customarily associated with multiple, disguised, contextual or ambiguous meanings. The trickster inhabits liminal zones and is perpetually travelling, lone and rootless. He (and historically he is invariably male) is asocial as well as amoral, traversing boundaries that constrain the rest of us, such as right and wrong, sacred and profane, clean and dirty, male and female, young and old, living and dead, valuable and banal. The transgression or confusion of these categories is not simply an act of malign destruction, but through creative play prompts constant revaluation, making possible the promotion of shit to riches and rubbish to beauty – or vice versa. This is a recognisable characterisation of the mischievous artist, and in *Magic Show* Christian Jankowski overtly enacts these tricksterish principles in the commercial world (see p. 74), subtly casting his sceptical gaze on the business of popular astrology, transmuting the authority of the oracle into the stuff of art.

The trickster is closely associated with the conman, who, like the coyote of Native American mythology, hoodwinks his fellows to fill his belly. Applying tricks developed from esoteric magical practices to the most secular of uses, the conman is an opportunist, performing sleights of hand in contingent circumstances, taking advantage of accidents and overly suggestive minds. The proximity of tricks and cons demonstrates the fine line between harmless fictions and toxic lies, indicating the fragility of the edges of epistemology. Wherever knowledge, truth, conviction and fabrication overlap, the well-placed word or covert action can wreak havoc with our ability to find any line at all. And just as it may be simplistic to ascribe 'truth' a higher moral position, it is also impossible to overlook the productive potential of lying. Lying involves obscuring what really happened with the representation of something that did not happen; it is a process of doubling, a bifurcation of possibilities. Perhaps it is this splitting of the world into two versions that makes lying so much more interesting, as it layers the actual and the possible, the fantastical and the mundane. Art is not in the business of giving information, dealing with facts or circulating truths; art is inherently duplicitous. When an artist makes a definitive statement, as in Friedman's cursed plinth, he has us over the barrel of irony. Irony, too, doubles the world, into what is said and what is meant. Irony makes it difficult to ascertain the status of a claim, particularly in a gallery, where artifice is law.

Even politically engaged artists, broadly speaking, do not give credence to objective truth or employ the approach of the investigative journalist. Rather than confronting questionable policies or outing falsehoods with evidence and affidavits, they are more likely to wield fiction as a rhetorical tool, throwing established power structures and hierarchies of knowledge into doubt by proposing fabulous alternatives. Nietzsche proclaimed that truths are illusions about which it has been forgotten that they *are* illusions, and the magician-artist might make this explicit by amplifying the artifice of existing information structures. Suzanne Treister, for instance, revisits the methods of the alchemist – the esoteric antecedent of the sceptical stage magician – and projects them on to the world of mass media, capitalism, global politics and technology (see p. 88). Her drawings imbue broadsheets and tabloids with magical potency, as if divining teleological cause behind events. Far from claiming belief in the supernatural, however, the contemporary artist appropriates such arcane imagery to undermine by inference those current power or knowledge structures that are widely and complacently accepted.

Like a briefcase with a false bottom, then, art contains more than may at first appear. It often sneaks difficult ideas past a cynical audience or springs surprising effects from mundane causes. Like Rick Buckley's sweet potato (see p. 55) – which has been exalted to cult status, standing for something significant that is held forever beyond our ken – magic props are traditionally banal and rarely singular: the hat, the cups, the ball, the pack of cards. Since the transformation of the apparently known is more instantly discernible, magic acts upon bland archetypes. Similarly, Brian Griffiths' conversion of dull pieces of furniture into artefacts of enchantment (see p. 65) exemplifies the artist's ability to find value in the ordinary and pull focus on the accidental or overlooked miracle. While not exactly devoid of intent, these miracles signal a turn away from the teleological towards the heroics of the everyperson. But is banality entirely eradicated and the quotidian valorised through these processes?

If we were to ask this question of secular magic, the answer would ultimately be 'no', as it makes no claim for real power over anything other than the audience's perception. And by assuming the methodologies of magic, artists too subscribe to a meta-fiction of power that is ultimately a narrative of bewilderment, instrumentalised to productive, disruptive or controlling ends.

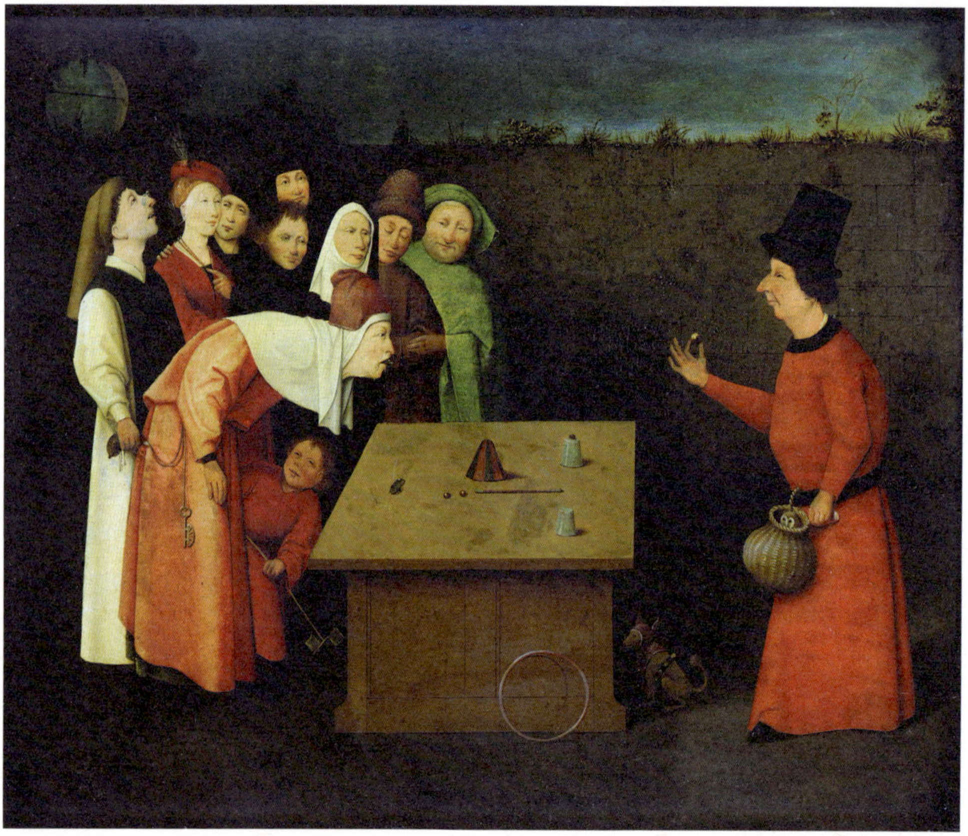

↑ Hieronymus Bosch (c.1450–1516), *The Conjurer*

From Bosch to Blackpool

JONATHAN ALLEN

FOR three days in late February the English coastal town of Blackpool hosts the world's largest convention of theatrical magicians, an international community of over three thousand professional, semi-professional and amateur practitioners who gather each year to catch up on the latest developments in the magic arts.

For those unfamiliar with the theatrical magic world, Blackpool's convention can be an overwhelming experience. Set within the maze of theatres and Spanish-themed conference halls that make up the city's Winter Gardens complex, the convention comprises a vast and highly specialised marketplace of ingenious gadgetry and recondite information, an extensive programme of lectures delivered by globe-trotting celebrity performers, historians and theorists, and a jostling competition circuit where magicians vie against one another for prized trophies and rosettes of professional merit. Although this panorama of illusioneering has emerged as the most well-attended international event of its kind, the Blackpool convention is just one facet of a larger network of affiliated and unaffiliated magic organisations worldwide. This landscape is dominated by the formidable International Brotherhood of Magicians (IBM), whose member groups are bound together through 'linking rings', a metaphorical badge of solidarity that it shares with its membership magazine, in print since January 1923.

Whenever I make the journey to Blackpool and view at close quarters the extensive network of expertise that congregates there each year, I am surprised anew that this ancient art form has attracted so little sustained critical attention from the academy. Theatrical magic's historical durability alone should make it a significant object of enquiry, whilst its *modus operandi*, which offers models for both the production and consumption of epistemologically precarious experience, provides grist to any number of critical mills, not least in the visual and performing arts. The exhibition *Zauberkünste* [Doing Magic] at the Nordico Museum in Linz in the spring of 2009 was the first in-depth historical survey of the figure of the theatrical magician, and marks a key moment in this respect.[1] Not that magicians themselves are culturally invisible; quite the reverse. In recent years, performers such as Derren Brown and David Blaine have enjoyed both live and mediated audiences that compare in scale to magic's so-called Golden Era (c.1890–1930), a period recently fictionalised in films such as Christopher Nolan's *The Prestige* (2006) and Neil Burger's *The Illusionist* (2006). The lexicon of theatrical magic is likewise ubiquitous, although all too often confused with its supernatural near-relation, magick. The descriptor 'magical' abounds culturally, in particular within commercial advertising, and, it should be noted, within the contemporary art world, where the ability of an artist to 'conjure' this or that is habitually presented by commentators as an unqualified guarantee of creative adroitness. Considerable economic and cultural capital thus attaches itself to magic's transformative appeal, with little acknowledgment of the latter's heterogeneity and complex cultural relations.

Two main factors have contributed to theatrical magic's critical estrangement: perception and access. In an era of rationalisation and bewildering technological interfaces, it is perhaps easy to dismiss the spectacle of a man (usually a man, but by no means always) standing on a stage pretending to work miracles, or, as was fashionable a few years ago, detaining and then entertaining the public with tricks on street corners with a camera crew close at hand. Magic's apparent triviality and gender bias are aggravated by suspicions of its duplicity. Since tactical deception and misdirection are technical pre-requisites for the conjuring arts, its proponents have historically been associated as much with devilry or charlatanism (if not downright criminality) as they have with artistry. Perhaps of more consequence for researchers than perception, however, have been the restrictions placed upon magic's archive by magicians themselves, who for aesthetic and economic reasons have carefully monitored the boundaries of their art. The code upheld by most magicians, neatly summed up by The Magic Circle's motto *Indocilis Privata Loqui* [Not apt to disclose secrets], has meant that significant chunks of theatrical magic's vast and revealing archive have, until only very recently, remained invisible to those on the ticket side of magic's tinselled curtain.

Despite this perceived cultural lightness, potential crookedness and problematised archive, the figure of the theatrical magician has attracted the positive regard of some within academia. In an essay for *Arts Journal* in 1993, Barbara Maria Stafford argued a case for 'remetaphorising' the marginalised figure of the conjuring 'empiric', noting that popular illustrated books such as Henri Decremps's *La Magie blanche dévoilée* [White Magic Unveiled] (1784) had offered the conjurer as a progressive and positive figure of enlightenment, rather than the more commonly dismissed mountebank who encourages 'passive gaping in the uncritically credulous'.[2] In 'Conjuring – How the Virtuoso Romantic Learned from the Enlightened Charlatan', Stafford writes:

> *conjuring was not just mindless spectacle but a force for visual education. Momentary concealment and subsequent revelation were not the same as a permanent lie. This fluid and interactive performance medium demonstrated that legerdemain, camouflage, distraction, misdirection, and above all the perspective one had, permeated the perception of life and need not be evil ... Invited to conceptualise or model generally practiced social strategies of deception, [the public], too, might eventually learn to avoid self-deception.*[3]

In 2001, James W. Cook extended Stafford's valorisation of this instrumentalised magic in *The Arts of Deception*, but also noted the surprising absence from mainstream academia of extended studies of 'the profane magical practices of the urban exhibition hall. It is almost as if academic historians have taken Max Weber's classic theory about the "disenchantment of the world" as a guide for assessing the social significance of the magician during the nineteenth and twentieth centuries'.[4] Indeed it is Max Weber's proposition that modernity leaves a disenchanted, rationalising secularity in its wake which provides the context for academia's most conspicuous and suggestive treatment of the theatrical magician to date, Simon During's *Modern Enchantments: The Cultural Power of Secular Magic* (2002).

In *Modern Enchantments* During sets out to establish a clear distinction between two constituently different but historically coexisting magics: magic that draws upon supernatural agency (its occult, shamanic and spiritualist traditions for instance, but also including the supernaturalism of mainstream religion), and magic that makes no claim, or no serious claim at least, to being in contact with supernatural forces. This 'secular magic' is the province of the theatrical conjurer but also the key component of a historical construct that During labels the 'magic-assemblage': 'that loose motley of shows in public spaces where magic was performed ... lantern shows or early film, feats of strength, juggling, posture mastery, ventriloquism, puppet shows, trained animal exhibitions, comic routines, automata displays, lotteries, and joy rides.'[5] It might be argued by binary theorists of historical development that this secularised form of magic simply replaced its supernatural predecessor in the West as Weber's 'disenchantment' took hold, but During shows that magic's story is considerably more complex: secular magic has co-existed and interacted with its 'opposing twin, magic with a supernatural punch' from (at least) antiquity and on through emergent and late modernity.[6] Hence our sense of magic's 'doubleness': on the one hand we call upon the idea of magic to articulate, if not instrumentalise, culture's most complex metaphysical formulations and transactions, and on the other hand use the same term to describe theatricalised shortcuts to the supernatural care of Las Vegas illusionists, or a few marvel-less props bought from a magic dealer in Blackpool.

Having teased out these two historically parallel but discrete magics, During argues that magic's secular form has been a far more significant force in the West than is commonly acknowledged. He demonstrates how conjuring displays and other elements of the magic assemblage helped carve out the cultural and commercial spaces later occupied by the modern entertainment industries (most conspicuously by contributing directly to the emergence of film), guiding curious and questioning subjects towards secularity at the same time as, or even in advance of, an academy-led scientific Enlightenment. Secular magic audiences could be understood thus to have embodied something akin to a lay enlightenment, because their experiences of conjuring displays and other forms of 'rational recreation' left them ultimately un-deluded as to the origin of their enchantment. Habituated by a compelling range of these 'modern enchantments', During's more self-conscious viewer complicates familiar accounts of Western modernity such as *Dialectic of Enlightenment* (Max Horkheimer and Theodor Adorno, 1947), and *Society of the Spectacle* (Guy Debord, 1967), indicating modernising subjects who, far from being overwhelmed by modernity's insidious and dehumanising spell, remain 'critical and ... under spectacle's spell simultaneously'.[7] Whereas Debord describes the spectacle as the domain of 'the deceived gaze and false consciousness ... the opposite of dialogue',[8] During argues that this viewing subject could be understood as considerably more capacitated than conventional dialectical accounts allow.

Although the critical academy has been slow to recognise the figure of the secular magician, let alone the more empowered subject *Modern Enchantments* describes, the same could not be said for magic's own peer-academy. Although magic's seminal history, *Lives of the Conjurers*, was written in 1876 by a non-magician, the ex-Chartist Thomas Frost, magic historians since have followed his model to capture magic's often anecdotal, not infrequently falsified, and thus potentially errant history.[9] *An Illustrated History of Magic* (Milbourne Christopher, 1973), *The Great Illusionists* (Edwin A. Dawes, 1979), *Those Beautiful Dames* (Frances Marshall and Amy Dawes, 1984), *Learned Pigs and Fireproof Women* (Ricky Jay, 1986) and *Hiding the Elephant* (Jim Steinmeyer, 2003) are conspicuous examples from a vast library of curtain-side histories that provide detailed and candid perspectives on secular magic's complex lineage. Magician-theorists likewise have been exacting within many volumes, such as *Our Magic* (Nevil Maskelyne and David Devant, 1911), and *Magic in Theory* (Peter Lamont and Richard Wiseman, 1998). This highly productive self-regard has come at some cost to the magic community, for the intensity of its singular gaze, combined with an inclination for secrecy, has for long periods of history minimised formal interpenetration from, although not informal collaboration with, other academic fields. Technology, however, has challenged this boundary. An emerging generation of practitioners and historians, first responding to the penetrating gaze of television, and now perhaps unable or unwilling to control the online distribution of magic's archive, have begun to adopt more pragmatic, even dialogical approaches. The recently published *Magic 1400s–1950s* (2009) evolved following collaborations between editor Noel Daniel and magic historians Mike Caveney, Jim Steinmeyer and Ricky Jay. The Conjuring Arts Research Center in New York, opened in 2003, is a further example. The door to magic history's library, and to some extent its technical workshop, is more invitingly open now than it has ever been.

The consequences of this increasing acquiescence are already beginning to be felt. A number of magicians including Teller, the silent half of the iconoclastic American duo Penn & Teller, recently formed part of a collaborative research project at the Barrow Neurological Institute in Phoenix, Arizona. The study focused on brain functioning principles understood intuitively and exploited by magicians for centuries, but little known within the scientific community, and the results were published in the respected *Nature Reviews Neuroscience* in September 2009. Magicians themselves, attending the Third European Conference of Magic History and Collections at Vienna's Naturhistorisches Museum, were addressed, and at times significantly challenged, by representatives of an unexpectedly diverse range of academic fields including ethnology, papyrology, cultural studies, contemporary art and etymology. Another consequence of magic's increasing receptivity has been a far greater sense of the magician's social, economic and even political influence as he or she reaches out and touches audiences far beyond the fourth wall. Conjurers have, for example, collaborated closely with governments during periods of warfare, and elsewhere behind the scenes on the international political stage.[10] The role of secular magic within religious (and other non-secular) rituals can be reassessed, given that the former is often interwoven almost indistinguishably with the latter in many traditional and contemporary contexts.[11] It is perhaps of less surprise that conjuring's lexicon and iconography can be found at play widely within commercial advertising – a 'conjuring of consent' one might say, to adapt Edward Bernays' infamous 'engineering of consent'. Here magic shares a stage with everything from breakfast cereal and shoe polish to birth control pills.[12] As technology has accelerated, and magicians have become less constrained, a more complete picture of the secular magician is emerging, a protean figure of historical complexity, socially, economically and often ideologically embedded, an elaborate and elaborating figure of cultural agency.

The question remains, however, as to why we might be interested in this particular form of magic in the first place given that, amongst many other culturally productive and instructive magics, theatrical magic is anything but unpopular. In *Beyond the Pleasure Principle*, Sigmund Freud observes the behaviour of a child who playfully vanishes and reappears small objects, while at the same time producing the sounds *fort* [gone], and *da* [there]. Freud relates this *fort/da* game to 'the child's great cultural achievement – the instinctual renunciation (that is, the renunciation of instinctual satisfaction) which he had made in allowing his mother to go away without protesting'.[13] The developing child's quest for greater control over his or her world is echoed in the single-word answer offered by magicians to the question of magic's appeal to us as adults: wonderment. We are captivated by the idea that nature's laws and the capriciousness of chance might not bind us quite as mortally as we imagine; faced with the apparent momentary suspension of such fetters, we are filled with wonder at the possibility. Magic is, in the words of Teller, 'the theatrical linking of a cause with an effect that has no basis in physical reality, but that – in our hearts – ought to.'[14]

The construction of the conditions of wonderment can, however, be undertaken for both benign and nefarious ends. Herein lies another clue to our fascination: our concern over the distinction between temporary illusion (from *illudare*, to play) and permanent deception (from *decipere*, to ensnare or trap). This concern can be easily heard in the mixture of curiosity and reproach following any magic performance, summed up in the question 'How did you *do* that?' The other question that is being asked here is, of course, 'How did *you* do that?' and perhaps even, '*Why* did you do that?' These are questions we habitually ask of other forms of constructed power that assemble the reality around us, be they governmental, legal, economic, scientific, religious or otherwise. Indeed, magicians in search of audiences have, historically, framed their performances within just these epistemologically volatile territories, where human fragility is most tellingly exposed. During eras of widespread religious belief, therefore, secular magicians in the West framed their performances with reference to Christendom's overarching systems of belief. The 15th century 'juggler' (as the secular magician was known until late in the 18th century) could never risk positive identification with diabolic confederacy, but might encourage crowds through risky proximity. Throughout more rationalising and industrialising periods, secular magicians shape-shifted into 'professors of science', aligning their conjuring displays with the cultural uncertainties stemming from the destabilising forces of scientific discovery. And in our own era, when we fear that the self might be reducible merely to the brain's chemical self-management, a magician such as Derren Brown is well-placed to tap our ontological anxieties, fears of being inadvertently controlled and even our desire to surrender our will altogether in the face of a troublingly indifferent universe. In a recent television appearance he explained that the show would fuse 'magic, suggestion, psychology, misdirection and showmanship',[15] but the show's framing and thus its operative power was located elsewhere, in his references throughout to academically plausible but fuzzy concepts such as 'the wisdom of crowds', 'deep maths' and 'perception without awareness', as well as other types of persuasion assumed to be culturally rife, including subliminal advertising, political propaganda and neuro-linguistic programming. Brown deftly repurposes these abstractions to construct mediated or live events that depend, in fact, upon the deployment of theatrical magic principles that are often many centuries old.

The power that the theatrical magician wields is simulated.[16] This is not simply to say that such magic is not real. Theatrical magic is certainly not real, in that it is not supernatural – a fact that all such magicians must eventually admit, no matter how much, or for how long, they might couch their performances within the rhetoric of the supernatural agency. The moment for that admission is of course a matter of theatrical timing, and may take anything from a second on stage to a lifetime, and sometimes comes even from beyond the grave, via technical secrets sealed in envelopes discovered in hidden compartments of domestic furniture, or through assistants, stagehands, or prop-makers finally free to communicate the extent of their role before the footlights or offstage. Yet once a 'natural', rather than 'supernatural', basis for theatrical magic is established, its undoubted ability to radically disorder our epistemological assumptions about the world can be understood in terms of the magician's capacity to establish and maintain a frame through which simulated power over natural causality is experienced as real. In this sense, therefore, this form of magic is not only secular, but also simulacral. And it is the intentional presence and infinite malleability of this reifying frame, whether in the form of narrative or other contingent means, that brings simulacral magic alongside its sibling arts, and not least the visual arts with which it now shares more conceptual territory than perhaps at any other time.

Theatrical magic and the visual arts have shared, of course, literal pictorial frames throughout art history, with the conjurer appearing alongside other figures of popular entertainment within engravings such as Hogarth's *Southwark Fair* (1734), and as a versatile satirical tool in many popular prints – Daumier's lithograph of the swindler Robert-Macaire (1839) being a conspicuous example. Although the earliest representation of the magician as a sleight-of-hand artist known to date is thought to be a scene within a cassone-painting by Giovanni di Francesco Toscani, *The Garden of Love* (c.1420–30) in the Berlin State Museum, Gemäldegalerie,[17] art history's most conspicuous depiction of such a scene is Hieronymus Bosch's *The Conjurer* (p. 16), a work that survives now only as a copy in the Musée Municipal in St. Germain-en-Laye. Bosch's paintings are subject to considerable speculation by art historians, due in part to the fact that, unlike many other paintings of the period, their iconography cannot be matched with an identifiable patron. One thesis, Jeffrey Hamburger's *'Bosch's "Conjuror": An Attack on Magic and Sacramental Heresy'* (1984), interprets the scene as an 'anti-mass', proposing a cautioning and moralising Bosch intent on associating pre-Reformation anxieties over heretical sacramental rites with diabolically assisted sorcery. The latter is represented by the lowly itinerant entertainer who leads souls to damnation and impecunity via a blasphemous communion using conjurer's cups and a handful of cork balls. The conjurer's fingers, fixed in a parody of the *iunctio digitis* (the gesture adopted by priests during the consecration of the host during the Catholic mass), and the toad of heresy issuing symbolically from the mouth of the conjurer's astonished victim, also blind to a nearby pickpocket, all lend tolerable credence to this iconographic decoding. Magic/art historian Volker Huber, however, notes that causing a toad to leap from a spectator's mouth (the key element of Hamburger's analysis) was a common conjuring trick during the period, and suggests that we should proceed with caution when assigning significance to Bosch's conspicuously magic-related imagery. Huber highlights instead the only work on the same theme confirmed as Bosch's own – an ink drawing in the Department of Graphic Arts in the Louvre, which depicts the commonplace scene of a convivial performer plying his trade to an expectant audience on the streets of 15th-century Netherlands. His point is that a working knowledge of secular magic's social history and often surprising visual conventions can offer art historians important interpretive material that can lead to very different iconographical readings.[18]

More than five hundred years, but just four hundred miles, from Bosch's native city of 's-Hertogenbosch, in Blackpool's Winter Gardens a small crowd has gathered in front of a table behind which a conjurer is causing small cork balls to appear, vanish and multiply beneath polished brass cups at the touch of a wand. Although most practitioners understand the misdirection required to accomplish these nimble sleights – indeed the mastery of a classic cups and balls routine is the magic equivalent of an article of faith through which an enthusiast becomes a devotee – even magicians themselves can be duped. Suddenly, mid-routine, the conjurer stops, and begins to fumble around on the tabletop with closed eyes as if searching for something lost. From beneath one of the cups, a pair of dark glasses is mysteriously discovered. The routine is supposed to develop with the elegant, if surprising, revelation of a large orange or lemon, so this increasingly unpredictable version is already tantamount to conjuring heresy. Now the remaining cups are located and tilted over. But they reveal neither the expected fruit, nor any of the previously used cork balls. Instead, staring up towards the audience, are two perfectly formed painted glass eyeballs. Before anyone has time to respond to this ludicrous dénouement, the conjurer transforms her wand into a long white cane and, now sporting dark glasses, wanders away from the table with convincing unsteadiness before vanishing into the crowds.

Notes

[1] *Zauberkünste – In Linz und der Welt* [Doing Magic – in Linz and the World], exh. cat., Nordico – Museum der Stadt Linz, 2009, curated by Brigitte Felderer.

[2] Barbara Maria Stafford, 'How the Virtuoso Romantic Learned from the Enlightened Charlatan', *Art Journal*, Summer 1993, p. 28.

[3] Ibid., p. 28.

[4] James W. Cook, *The Arts of Deception*, Harvard University Press, Cambridge, Mass. and London, 2001, p. 166.

[5] Simon During, *Modern Enchantments: The Cultural Power of Secular Magic*, Harvard University Press, Cambridge, Mass. and London, 2002, p. 66.

[6] Ibid., p. 2.

[7] Simon During, 'Modern Enchantments: An Interview with Simon During/Sina Najafi', *Cabinet*, no. 26, Summer 2007, pp. 88-95.

[8] Guy Ernest Debord, *The Society of the Spectacle*, 1967, trans. Fredy Perlman and Jon Supak, Black & Red, Detroit, 1970, Chapter 1, sections 3 and 18.

[9] An ex-Chartist, Frost's motivation for chronicling performers in *Lives of the Conjurers* (1876) and *Old Showmen* (1874) was primarily political, aiming to improve the working conditions of, and to gain political representation for, otherwise socially and economically marginalised groups.

[10] Jonathan Allen, 'Deceptionists at War', *Cabinet*, no. 26, Summer 2007, pp. 65-72.

[11] See Randall Styers, *Making Magic: Religion, Magic, and Science in the Modern World*, AAR, Oxford 2004, and Jonathan Allen, 'Gospel Magic', *Contemporary*, no. 68, 2004.

[12] 'The engineering of consent is the very essence of the democratic process, the freedom to persuade and suggest.' Edward L. Bernays, 'The Engineering of Consent', *Annals of the American Academy of Political and Social Science*, March 1947. See also Jim Hagy, *Magic for Free*, Reginald Scot Books, Glenview, 2006.

[13] Sigmund Freud, *Beyond the Pleasure Principle*, 1920, *Standard Edition* vol. 18, pp. 14-15.

[14] Teller, 'Sleights of Mind', *New York Times*, 21 Aug. 2007.

[15] Derren Brown, 'The Events – How to Control The Nation', first broadcast 18 Sept. 2009, Channel 4.

[16] Jean-Eugène Robert Houdin's description of theatrical magic as 'l'art de la magie simulée', was translated by Professor Hoffmann as 'fictitious magic' in *The Secrets of Conjuring and Magic or How to Become a Wizard*, Routledge, London, 1878.

[17] For many years, the earliest known depiction of a secular magician was thought to be an illuminated manuscript titled *The Children of the Planets, Luna* by Joseph of Ulm, dated 1404 (Libr. Univ. of Tübingen). This dating has been called into question by Dieter Blume, who indicates 1475 as a more accurate origination date (D. Blume, *Regenten des Himmels. Astrologische Bilder im Mittelalter und Renaissance* [Regents of the Heavens: Astrological Images of the Middle Ages and Renaissance], Akademie Verlag, Berlin, 2000). I am grateful to Pierre Taillefer for indicating these revised historical timelines.

[18] In *Gibecière: The Journal of The Conjuring Arts Research Centre*, vol.3, no.1, Winter 2008, Volker Huber comments on two works by Max Beckmann, *Magic Mirror* (1946) and *Three Headed Woman* (1946), both much elaborated upon by art historians. Huber demonstrates that the source of the iconography within each of these enigmatic compositions can be identified as popular Victorian stage illusions.

Illuminating Magics

A Resonant Moment in the Twinned Histories of Art and Magic

SIMON DURING

In Paris, on 10 June 1912, Marcel Duchamp attended a play, *Impressions d'Afrique*, by the little-known author Raymond Roussel. What he saw was a series of spectacles and strange contraption-produced illusions presented, so the fiction went, by a group of shipwrecked Europeans for the investiture of a tyrannical African king. Later Duchamp – who was a fan of popular spectacle, becoming a manufacturer of optical illusion machines himself, and, indeed, dreaming up a moneymaking scheme to sell magical fetish objects – was to recall that the event struck him with all 'the madness of the unexpected'.

Roussel, he declared, was 'responsible for' his own magnum opus, *The Bride Stripped Bare by Her Bachelors Even*, a Rousselean contraption (an 'instrument for farming'), which Duchamp began working on soon after seeing the play. It is likely, too, that Duchamp's first 'readymade' – the *objet trouvé* with which, in 1916, he broke down the barriers between art and everyday life, and thereby paved the way for the 20th-century art world – was, in a certain sense, a portrait of Roussel. At least, as a bicycle wheel [*roue*] mounted on a stool [*selle*], it played on Roussel's name. So it is no surprise that Duchamp, after whom art came to encompass whatever experiences, objects and thoughts the art-world designated as 'art', was later to declare that his ideal library 'would have contained all Roussel's writings'.

Roussel himself was mad about magic. His fictions describe mechanical devices and illusions that are more wonderful than any we will ever see in this world. But they themselves do so mechanically. Roussel's writing mimics the illusion-producing implements that his characters invent: he generated his best texts using a secret set of homophonic procedures that arbitrarily determined which phrases could complete particular sections of prose. This mechanical technique is what triggered Duchamp's intense and animating admiration for him.

In the end, Roussel pronounced that literature and art are dedicated to effects whose power (whether of wonder, representation, wisdom, delight, awe, curiosity, imitation, intoxication or surprise) necessarily exceeds its means, simply because those means are mechanical and formal rather than inspirational or spiritual. Invention is expressed in devices and illusions are effects – never more so than when Duchamp declares a urinal a work of art or a stage magician astonishes through machines of illusion and sleight of hand.

That is why the modern categories 'art' and 'secular magic' cannot be imagined except as bound together. Art may be serious and profound while magic is trivial and light. Art may generate immense cultural capital while magic generates almost none. Art may require sophisticated training to fully appreciate it while magic works well on those who know nothing. Art may be for adults and magic for kids. But in the end they are produced from the same trick, the same deception and the same logic: the trick by which an effect is consecrated as more than it is; the deception of not revealing (or not being able to reveal) quite how the trick was pulled off; the logic that enables something to be invented from nothing much.

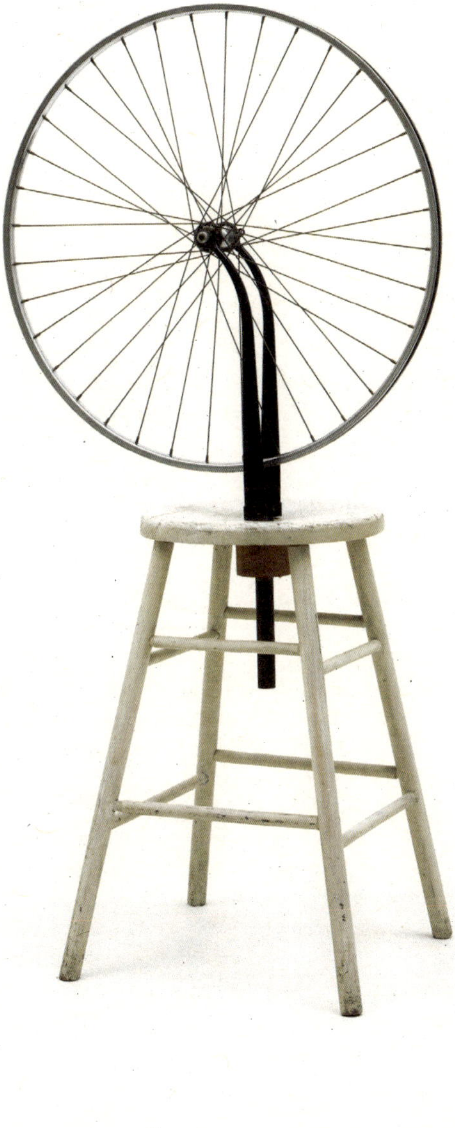

↑ Marcel Duchamp, *Bicycle Wheel*, 1951 after lost original of 1913

Headless

BRIGITTE FELDERER

The scenario is well-known: the man in tails and top hat commands the scene, conjuring things out of thin air and making them disappear, drawing onto the stage whomever he chooses from the audience. He controls, manipulates, destroys and creates. The woman at his side is no lady of refinement but a glamorous assistant, reassuring eye-candy ready to assist the master of ceremonies. She passes the magic wand, disposes of the umbrellas, confetti and garlands that have appeared, draws back curtains and lets them fall, portrays wonder before there is anything to wonder at. She is an animated ornament, and that seems to be her only role. She does not advise or interfere. Her admiring smiles and applause make the magician appear more credible, more manly and superior – living proof that the magician's powers go beyond magic.

Her actual complicity remains concealed, however. While her prettiness seems like decoration for decoration's sake, all eyes are on her; and it is this that enables her to distract and fool the audience, thereby playing a fundamental part in the tricks being performed. Magic tricks that enlist a woman operate by the very fact that, for the duration of the trick, gender-based stereotyping are apparent to everyone in the audience, but as the magician deceives the intellect by letting us see what we want to see, the audience becomes simultaneously prey to and seduced by its own fantasies and desires.

But these clichés shouldn't obstruct our view of history. Female magicians knew long before their male counterparts how to make the most of gender stereotypes in their art. Before the first virginal victim was sawn in two in the 20th century, female magicians were already well versed in manipulation of the audience's belief and confidence. Artists like Caroline Bernhardt – legendary for a trick in which her own leg was torn from her body – demonstrated in the early 19th century that the only way to hoodwink reason was to engage with both rational assumptions and the desire for illicit thrills. In 1846 'Professor' Bernhardt announced that she wished to execute a beheading on stage and would then, 'for the instruction of the young', even go so far as to explicate the trick. The advertisement for the event shows the artist holding a sword in one hand and a platter balancing the freshly severed head of a man in the other. Bernhardt was a true professional: what she grasped absolutely was that the figure of the magician, the artist, was as important to the triumphant realisation of an illusion as the actual mechanics of the trick. Revealing the details of a trick does not, after all, reveal its effect. This decapitation-practicing 'recipient of the Medal for Merit in Art and Science' very knowingly invited both Eros and Death to the stage, giving life to the illusion even before delving into her box of tricks.

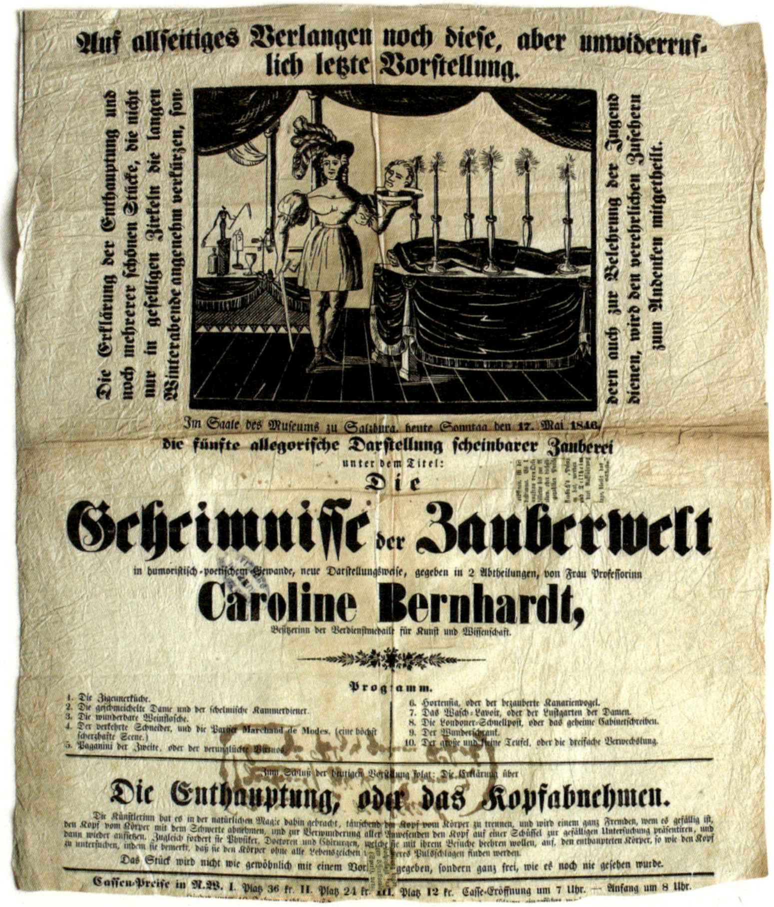
Auf allseitiges Verlangen noch diese, aber unwiderruflich letzte Vorstellung.

Die Erklärung der Enthauptung und noch mehrerer schönen Stücke, die nicht nur in geselligen Zirkeln die langen Winterabende angenehm verkürzen, sondern auch zur Belehrung der Jugend dienen, wird den verehrlichen Zusehern zum Andenken mitgetheilt.

Im Saale des Museums zu Salzburg, heute Sonntag den 17. Mai 1846,
die fünfte allegorische Darstellung scheinbarer Zauberei
unter dem Titel:
Die
Geheimnisse der Zauberwelt
in humoristisch-poetischem Gewande, neue Darstellungsweise, gegeben in 2 Abtheilungen, von Frau Professorinn
Caroline Bernhardt,
Besitzerinn der Verdienstmedaille für Kunst und Wissenschaft.

Programm.

1. Die Zigeunerküche.
2. Die geschmeichelte Dame und der schelmische Kammerdiener.
3. Die wunderbare Weinflasche.
4. Der verkehrte Schneider, und die Pariser Marchand de Modes. (eine höchst scherzhafte Scene.)
5. Paganini der Zweite, oder der verunglückte Virtuos.
6. Hortensia, oder der bezauberte Kanarienvogel.
7. Das Wasch-Lavoir, oder der Lustgarten der Damen.
8. Die Londoner-Schnellpost, oder das geheime Cabinetschreiben.
9. Der Wunderschrank.
10. Der große und kleine Teufel, oder die dreifache Verwechslung.

Zum Schluß der heutigen Vorstellung folgt: Die Erklärung über
Die Enthauptung, oder das Kopfabnehmen.
Die Künstlerinn hat es in der natürlichen Magie dahin gebracht, täuschend den Kopf vom Körper zu trennen, und wird einem ganz Fremden, wem es gefällig ist, den Kopf vom Körper mit dem Schwerte abnehmen, und zur Verwunderung aller Anwesenden den Kopf auf einer Schüssel zur gefälligen Untersuchung präsentiren, und dann wieder aufsetzen. Zugleich fordert sie Physiker, Doctoren und Chirurgen, welche sie mit ihrem Besuche beehren wollen, auf, den enthaupteten Körper, so wie den Kopf zu untersuchen, indem sie bemerkt, daß sie den Körper ohne alle Lebenszeichen [illegible] Pulsschlagen finden werden.
Das Stück wird nicht wie gewöhnlich mit einem Vor[illegible] gegeben, sondern ganz frei, wie es noch nie gesehen wurde.

Cassen-Preise in C.M. I. Platz 36 kr. II. Platz 24 kr. III. Platz 12 kr. Casse-Eröffnung um 7 Uhr. — Anfang um 8 Uhr.

↑ Broadside advertising a performance by Caroline Bernhardt ‘in the hall of the museum in Salzburg, today, Sunday 17th May 1846’

Magic and the willing suspension of disbelief

PETER LAMONT

If you go to the theatre and see Peter Pan flying above the stage, you ignore the wires: that is a willing suspension of disbelief. If you go to the theatre and see David Copperfield flying above the stage, you do not ignore the wires. You look for the wires. You do not see any wires. That is magic.

If you look for the wires and see them, that is bad magic. If you do not look for the wires because the possibility has not occurred to you, then you do not need magic since you must live in a world of endless wonders. If the possibility of wires does occur to you but you decide not to look for them, then that is indeed a willing suspension of disbelief. But it is not magic.

We are not talking here about the magic of theatre, or the magic of literature, prose or poetry. Of course, we can be transformed or transported by these, as one can by a sunset, a flower or a mountain view. We are talking here about conjuring effects, the apparently impossible events that rely upon the esoteric methods of the magician. Magic is neither theatre nor fiction, in that whatever theatrical or fictional elements might be involved, the essence of magic is that something impossible appears to happen in real time and space. To truly experience an impossible event, you must observe an event that you truly believe to be impossible. A willing suspension of disbelief can only diminish that experience.

For example, perhaps the impossible event is that an object vanishes. This requires that you observe that it was there, but is no longer there. It should not involve any suspension of disbelief. On the contrary, it requires a genuinely held belief that what you are seeing prior to the magical effect is really happening (that the object really is there), or else the effect (that it is no longer there) cannot work. This belief is not willingly suspended disbelief; it is belief based on observable evidence. The more convincing this evidence (i.e. the more convinced you are that the object really is there), the stronger the magical effect (when you see that it has gone). The strength of the effect is directly proportional to the belief (not willingly suspended disbelief, but genuine real-time conviction) that the object truly was where it was supposed to be. This is the primary aim of magic as a performing art: the creation of a juxtaposition between the conviction that something cannot happen and the observation that it just happened. It requires disbelief (that it can happen) based on a conviction (that, in these conditions, it is impossible) in order for the effect (but it just happened) to produce the experience. In short, if you suspend disbelief, the magic disappears.

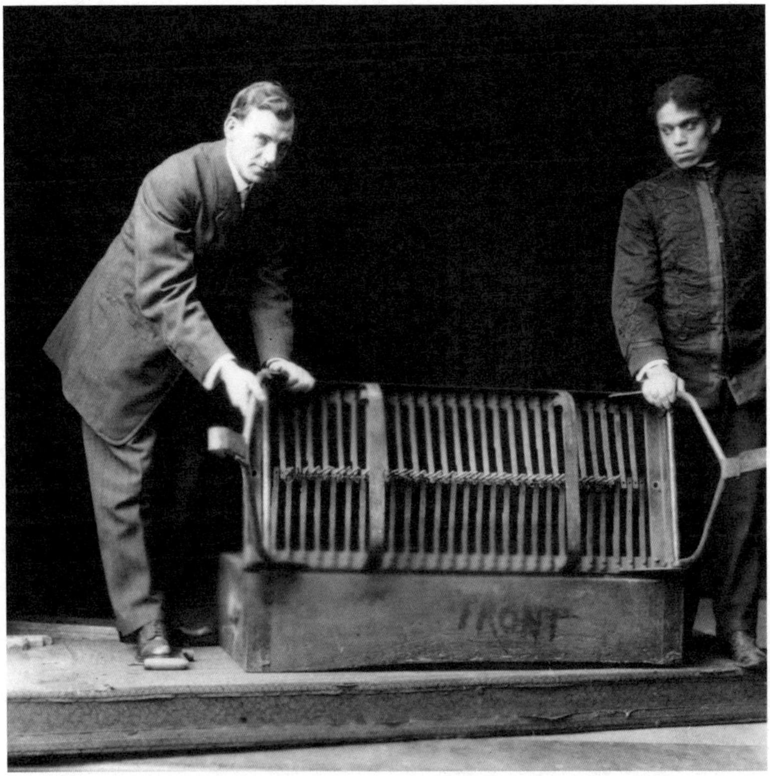

↑ Photograph from Howard Thurston's 'Workbooks' (c. 1910-11), in which the American magician documented the technical aspects of his show, including the apparatus (partly seen here) used to create the most celebrated illusion of its time, 'The Levitation of Princess Karnac' (also known as 'The Maskeleyne/Kellar Levitation').

Pebbles in the Polis

PIERRE TAILLEFER

Pebbles [*psēphoi*] were the ancient Greek conjurer's most common prop. As described by Artemidorus (2nd century AD) in his treatise on dream interpretation: 'He makes the pebbles [*psēphous*] disappear, and then makes them reappear here and there'. This trick defined conjuring to such an extent that the pebble came to symbolically designate the conjurer, both verbally and visually.

This metonymy was engrained in the words themselves. The Greek for conjurer was either 'pebble-player' [*psēphopaiktēs*] or 'pebble-thief' [*psēphokleptēs*], as evident in Athenaeus's report of a Greek city where there was 'raised a bronze statue in the theatre of the conjurer [*psēphokleptou*] Theodorus, holding a pebble [*psēphon*] in his hand'. The pebble alone sufficed to represent his craft.

Both 'pebble-player' and 'pebble-thief' offer a key to understanding the history of conjurers. The history of magic as a game is tightly linked to a history of magic as theft. Artemidorus acknowledges this ambiguity by adding that 'when one is dreaming he is conjuring [*psēphopaiktein*], it means he will reap large benefits thanks to trickery and lies'.

In antiquity, however, the primary use of pebbles was not conjuring, but voting. The Greek *psēphoi* were used as ballots in elections and verdicts in trial decisions and, consequently, the Greek word for vote was *psēphos*. White pebbles designated a favourable vote and black ones condemnation, an echo of which can be found in the contemporary English verb 'to blackball'. The same practice occurred in Rome, where stones used in conjuring tricks and decision-making were called *calculi*.

In the ancient world there were some instances of manipulated votes, insofar as a specific name was coined by Sophocles for the person who manipulates a ballot: *psēphopoios*, or one who 'devises pebbles' for fraudulent purposes. Because of this similarity between words, we are naturally led to compare the art of the pebble-player with mishandled voting systems; and in his commentaries on writers of antiquity, Eustathius of Thessalonica (12th century AD) makes a connection between the words 'pebble-thief' [*psēphokleptēs*] and 'man arranging votes' [*psēphopoios*].

And so the conjurer – as in the 'pebble-player' or 'pebble-thief' – plays not with a mere pebble, but with the symbol of the city's authority. In his work on etymology, Julius Pollux (2nd century AD) mentions a fragment of a lost speech by Lysias (5th century BC) that uses the accusatory phrase 'to conjure justice' [*psēphopaiktousi to dikaion*] – literally, *to play pebbles with justice*. This new etymological perspective clarifies the otherwise ambiguous position of the thief-conjurer in the ancient city. Should we call our conjurer 'ballot-player' or 'ballot-thief'? Or should we consider him to be holding a mirror up to society's corruption, his act of concealment precipitating revelations?

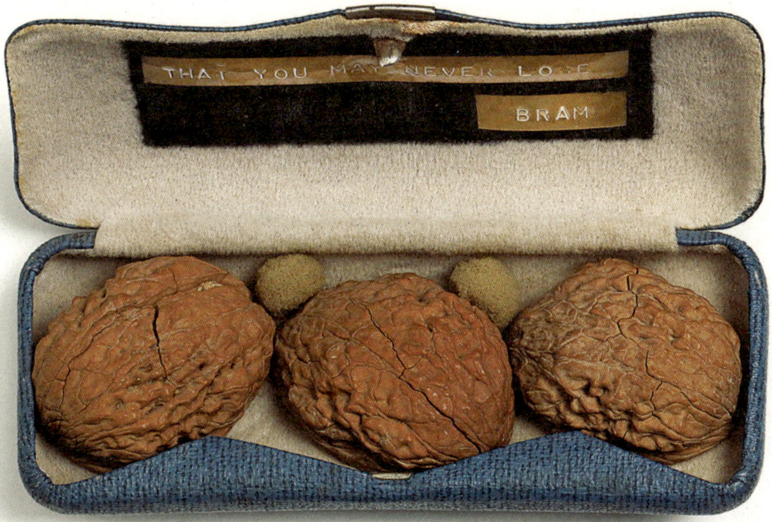

↑ Spectacles case containing reinforced walnut shells and sponge balls used to perform the shell game, a miniaturised street variation of the cups and balls trick. The inside lid displays the text 'THAT YOU MAY NEVER LOSE / BRAM', a message from the prop's previous owner, Dutch magician Abraham 'Bram' Pieter Adrianus Bongers, otherwise known as Fred Kaps (1926–80).

Ose's Leap into the Void

HELEN VAROLA

A photograph in *Genii* magazine from 1967 shows a cigar-hugging Man Ray at the Magic Castle, the invited guest of close-up performer Jay Ose. It was the year of Ose's death and the year after Ray's solo exhibition at the LA County Museum of Art. Ose is performing the gun trick, in which Ray's selected card, the nine of hearts, leaps into the air from a pistol-shaped deck of cards.

The Castle, as it is known to its mainly magician membership, was opened in the Hollywood hills in January 1963 by William Jr and Milton Larsen, with Ose as the club's first resident magician. *Genii*, then just 31 years old but destined to become the world's longest-running independent magic magazine in continuous publication, reviewed monthly events at the turreted gothic Victorian mansion in a column entitled 'Knights at The Magic Castle'. Writer Lou Derman noted: 'Jay Ose continues to delight and amaze Castle visitors with fifty-two honest cards and two cheatin' hands. Beyond selling his tricks, Jay sells himself – and to date nobody has yet asked for a refund.'

In small adverts on the pages that surround the photograph of the duo, other magicians sell and seek out magical effects. Calvert Products Co announce 'The Vanishing or Appearing Beer Bottle (Only $2.25 postpaid)'. Bob Rossi requests 'Dunninger's "The Elements of Mindreading" and "The Unconscious Conscious" (Please state condition and price)'. Meanwhile, the sardonic caption beneath the photograph reflects *Genii*'s informal and hierarchy leveling editorial tone: 'Jay Ose entertains famous artist Man Ray at the Magic Castle'. The photographer, perhaps an in-house employee and presumably tipped off as to the art-world celebrity status of one of the guests that evening, remains unnamed.

Experienced and opportunistic before the lens, Ose performs directly to camera. Ray's focus, however, seems to be fixed on the conceptual trigger of the illusion instead of the nine of heart's choreographed acrobatics. A master in encrypting coded messages, he gazes at the source of his potential bewilderment to identify any movement that might contain its secret.

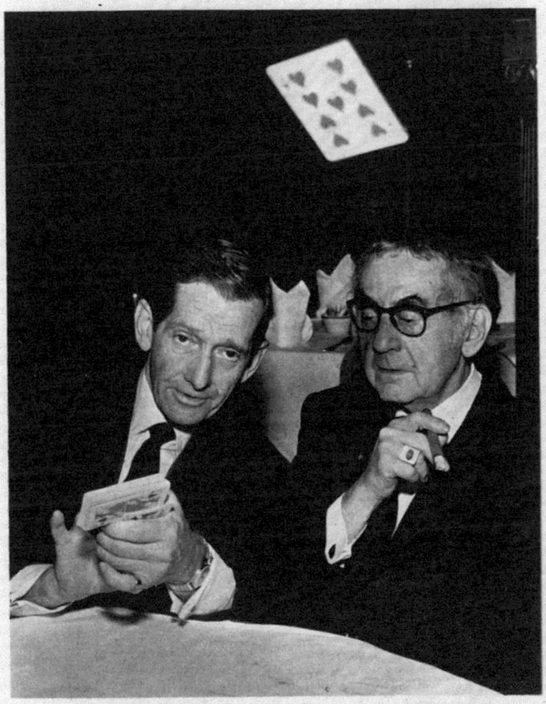

Jay Ose entertains famous artist Man Ray at the Magic Castle.

↑ Jay Ose and Man Ray at the Magic Castle, 1967

Death Charm

MARINA WARNER

Love spells cast in Surrey in the last century; a witch in a bottle from Sussex, found in 1926; and a lemon made in 1891 to bring about the death of a certain Mr William Smith, a greengrocer in Naples. All are displayed in the Pitt Rivers Museum, Oxford, alongside Chinese wax figures stuck with pins, shamanic crowns and Sarawak spirit wands. In the section called 'Magic and Superstition', and throughout this Victorian Wunderkammer, items are arranged strictly according to function: fishing tackle from all over the world in one place; smoking gear in another. At the time, this classification system was innovatory, even revolutionary: it abolished hierarchy and Eurocentrism and revealed, along evolutionist lines, that human beings everywhere came up with the idea of pitchforks, fish hooks, baskets, pots – and spells and charms.

Magic embeds desires in things. Once imbued with power, they acquire different names: relic, icon, talisman, amulet. The lemon from Naples, studded with 24 hob nails and six other wire nails, was found on the top of a window frame during a spring-cleaning, and was immediately recognised as a '*Fattura della morte*' [death spell]. The museum label continues: '...the servants refused to stay in the house with it and were terrified. ...Mrs Smith gave it to the depositor...' (We are not told when the unfortunate Mr Smith died.)

The lemon looks like a grenade, so called after the pomegranate; and it acts as a kind of a pomander, another citrus fruit, stuck with cloves to deal death to moths. But if its story didn't come with the impeccable authority of the scholarly British collector, Mr Eustace Neville-Rolfe, the lemon could be taken for a nail fetish [*nkisi nkongo*] from Zaire, one of those human and animal figures studded with metal till they bristle alarmingly. Do they work on the principle of sympathetic magic, according to which the action aims to procure the same at a distance, yet more intensely, so that by stabbing a lemon, the greengrocer will feel the same piercing agony? Anthropologists today reject this pop voodoo approach. They propose instead that such an object acts like a *pharmakon*, the subject of Derrida's meditations on writing. Enchanted by a form of inscription, the innocuous lemon has been engraved with meaning like a cuneiform tablet or a parchment impressed by a stele or quill. A fruit-bomb, a death charm, the lemon is replete with magical ambivalence, at once a remedy and a poison, bound fast by interlaced strings and transformed, by the nails and wishes driven into it, into a fearsome thing where few would feel comfortable to find their name.

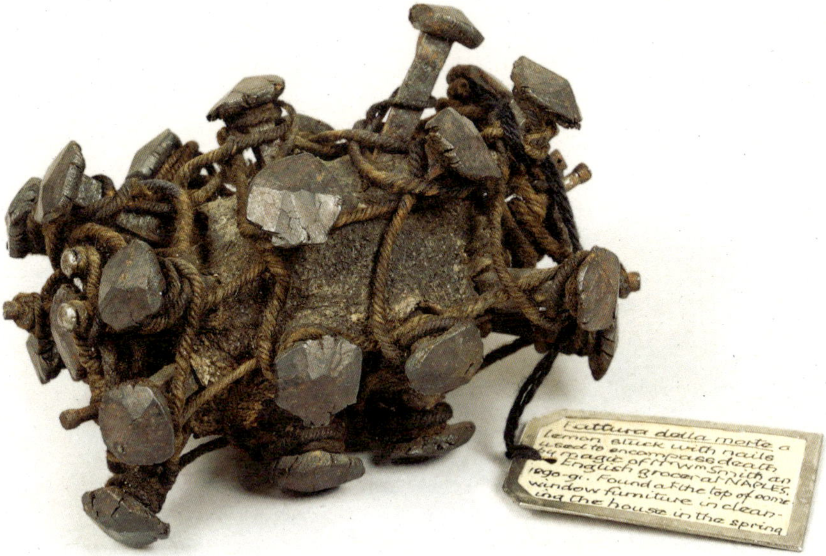

↑ *Fattura della morte* [Death Charm], c.1891

Wonderlust

In the following pages we tour through a century of literature and imagery to investigate the overlapping influences of magic, art and power. By way of short linking phrases, which indicate major underlying concepts, we discover how the world of thought and action are interconnected in unexpected ways.

To convey the essence and particularities of the text sources their idiosyncrasies of language and syntax have been left intact.

João Maria Gusmão & Pedro Paiva

Susan Hiller

Alexandra Hopf

Christian Jankowski

Janice Kerbel

Annika Lundgren

Juan Muñoz

Bruce Nauman

Ian Saville

Ariel Schlesinger

Suzanne Treister

Sinta Werner

Jonathan Allen

KALANAG was the stage name of Helmut Schreiber (1903–63), a magician and film producer deeply ensconced within the Nazi party during the Second World War, performing to many high-ranking officers including the Führer himself. The papier-mâché heads that hove into bifurcated view in Jonathan Allen's *Kalanag Double* (2009) are the actual props used by Kalanag during his world-touring stage show in the years following the war. They were to be worn by stand-ins who would briefly appear on stage, duping audiences into supposing that they had glimpsed the spectacular materialisation of the magician himself. In Allen's doppelganger portrait we are afforded an opportunity, for the first time, to cross-examine these heads, the crudeness of their caricature and their scars from years of usage.

We should perhaps shudder before these ciphers for conflicting genres of power, as Kalanag contaminated the figure of the benign entertainer with the nefarious potential of powers deployed to misdirect consent or facilitate coercion. Through a dialogical process of research and production, Allen habitually throws a revelatory political light on to the magic stage, and upon other platforms where ideological power is played out through stylisation, engineered perception or rhetorical display. His performance alter-ego, the 'gospel magician' Tommy Angel, for instance, outs the calculated choreography of the evangelical preacher, demonstrating how, through gesture and iconography, confidences are won through illusion and enticement in many a public domain.

As a member of The Magic Circle, Allen is uniquely placed to instigate pluralising conversations between the art, magic and other performative communities. His own performance and photographic work seeks out productive oscillations between illusion and disillusion, theatrically reconstructing the infusion of wonder and disquiet that pervades private and public life. The insubstantial or distinctly wobbly nature of authoritative structures, such as church, museum or government, is made particularly apparent through Allen's unstable media and imagery. From lenticular photographs of museum interiors in *Second Truths* (1998), whose contents switch allegiance as the viewer moves from side to side, to ruminations on breath in the mixed-media installation *Hot Air* (1993), where the very substance of life is seen to dissipate and elude scrutiny, knowledge is discerned as contingent and the facticity of the image defunct.

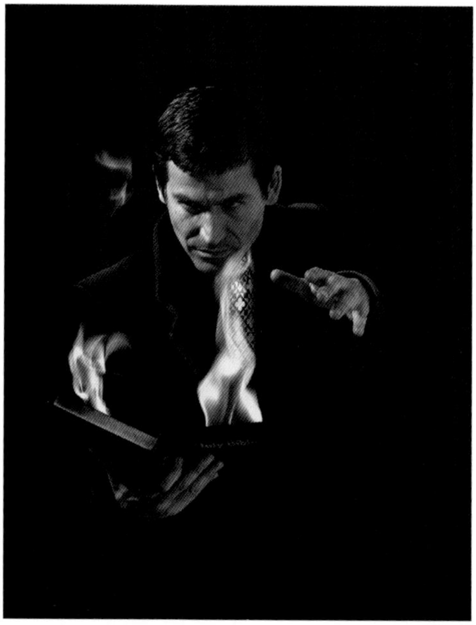

↑ *Tommy Angel #1*, 2005
→ *Kalanag Double*, 2009

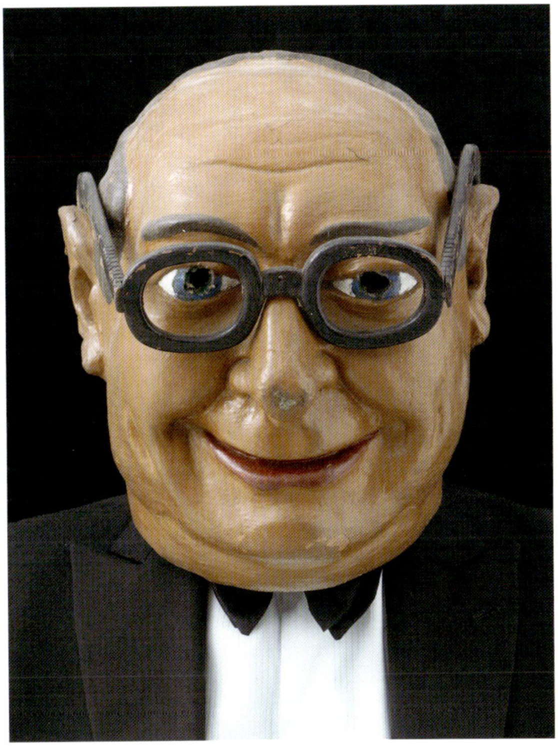

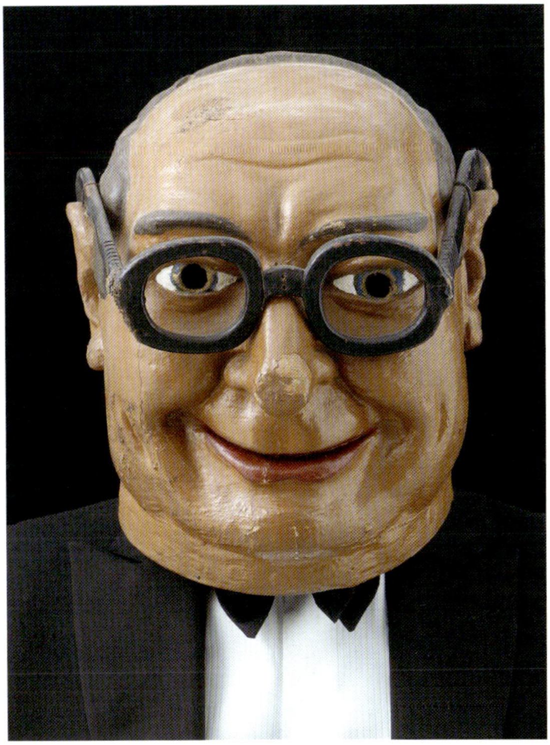

Archive
(Chris Kubick & Anne Walsh)

For their audio work *Yves Klein Speaks!* (2002), Archive invited mediums to contact the spirit of Yves Klein while in the presence of some of his works in private and institutional collections. Working from the premise that an artwork will be imbued with a spiritual residue, thereby enabling contact, the mediums are at times 'possessed' by Klein's spirit, while at others he appears as if a text from which to discern his appearance, read his character and translate his presence into spoken word.

For Archive, the séance is an allegory for the processes of revelation and secrecy, invention and reinvention that constitute history. Biographies, they suggest, are no different to other fantastical narratives, and autobiography, as a representation of the self, is no less theatrical than other performances. With this in mind, the wider series of séance-based works *Art After Death* takes as its subject artists who problematise notions of identity or self-awareness through masquerade, role-playing, passing or conning, such as Joseph Cornell (1903–72) and the 19th-century Italian self-portrait photographer Virginia Verasis, Countess of Castiglione (1837–99).

The performance of speech, as an extension of fictionalised self-representation, is an intricate affair that has lead Archive to consider such notions as translation (especially across media), subjectivity and mimesis, similarity and difference, collaborative identity, the library, the index and the archive. In a recent video work, *Lincoln in Tijuana* (2009), the artists worked with the Mexican magician-mentalist Nemonico, who performed a mind-reading trick in which he claimed to use a statue of Abraham Lincoln to channel thought. As Archive put it, it is of little consequence whether paranormal techniques are hoaxes or not, as 'the magic of belief and narrative is far more important than any matter of veracity'. For them, the important outcome of the project was to gain insight into the history of the relationship between the United States and Mexico, when the countries traded statues of Lincoln and Benito Juárez, then president of Mexico. The magician's use of Lincoln's statue, itself a symbol of mutual goodwill, transforms it into a cipher for limitless communication, encircling the historical with a metafiction of the improbable.

→ *Nemonico at the Lincoln statue*, Tijuana, Mexico, 2008

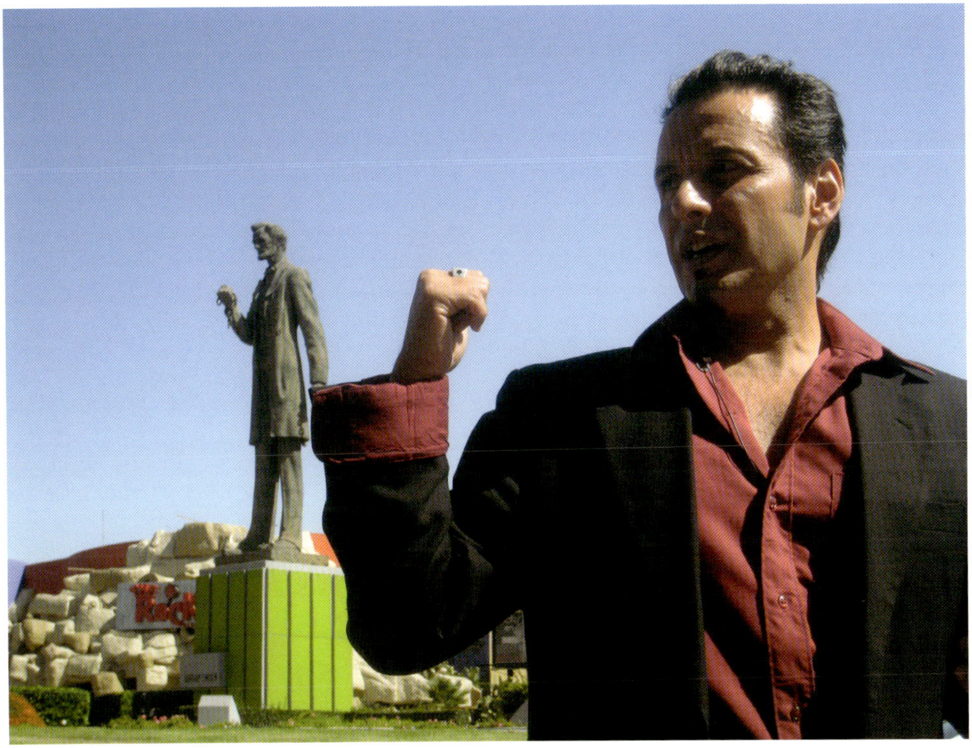

Zoe Beloff

Zoe Beloff's 3D video installation *A Modern Case of Possession* (2007) features an operatic performance, devised and adapted by the artist from an early 20th-century case study by the psychopathologist Pierre Janet. In supernatural terminology, a man appears to be possessed by a devil that compels him to shout obscenities and behave outrageously; in psychoanalytic terms, his condition is described as displaced guilt following an uncharacteristic adulterous episode. Beloff's translation of this early example of a scientific approach to mental health into a fully theatricalised operetta formalises the melodramatic potential of such a state, while its technology draws associations with hallucination or the ephemerality of dreams.

The apparatus that brings this sepulchral scene into view can be thought of as the technological progeny of the stereoscope, which was used to conjure spectres from thin air and scare the wits out of Victorian audiences. Whereas a 19th-century audience might have mistaken the virtual image for part of real, experiential space, Beloff's model theatre reinserts it into the representational space of the stage, creating a complex layering of perceptual registers, from the actual to the virtual to the delusional, as well as behavioural modes, from the compulsive to the performed.

Beloff's films and installations pose questions around the visualisation of mental states and the status of such images, as education or pure entertainment, or as prompters of fictions and preconceptions that indicate deeper social tendencies. In the installation *Dreamland* (2009) she presents films, drawings and maquettes for an amusement park devoted to the ideas of Sigmund Freud, where the 'Train of Thought' carries visitors around attractions and rides such as fun-house 'Mirrors of the Mind' and bumper cars driven by hysterical, infantilising or sadistic impulses. Reuniting science and spectacle in the vernacular of the music hall and sideshow, Beloff redrafts hallucination, psychosis, memory and desire with a black humour informed by a century of technology and analysis.

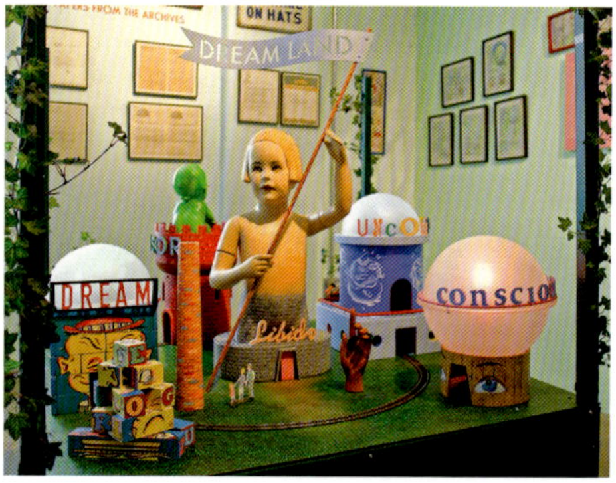

↑ *A restored model of Albert Grass's proposed Dreamland amusement park*, 2009 (detail)

→ *A Modern Case of Possession*, 2007 (video still)

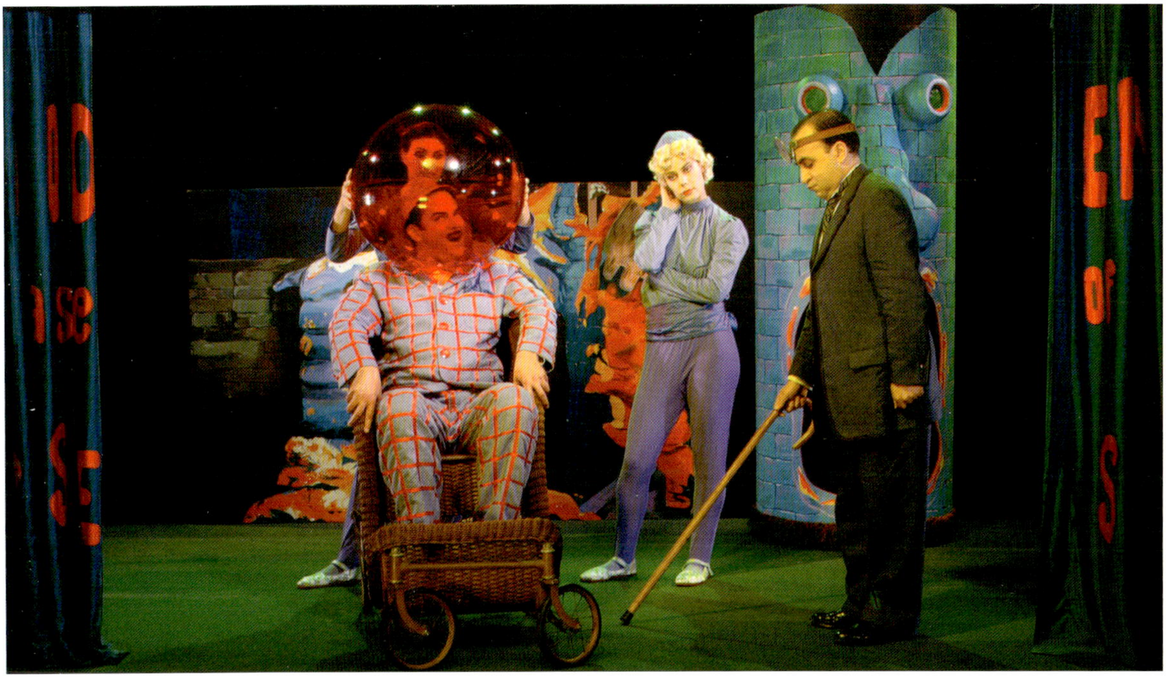

Ansuman Biswas & Jem Finer

Two apprentices of an ancient mystic sect have infiltrated the Cosmonaut Training Programme in Moscow and gained access to the zero gravity flight module. At the apex of a parabolic flight, before the plane begins its descent back to Earth, its pull is temporarily suspended, and it is under these conditions that the two turbaned men hope to lift off under the fuel of their well-packed hookah and practice piloting their magic carpet.

The absurd fiction of *Zero Genie* underpins the very corporeal image of two men in the archetypal dress of the middle-eastern mystic buffeting about the interior of a Russian cargo plane – an incongruity that unravels yet another epic narrative. The contrast between contemporary technology and the exoticised stereotype chimes with the perceived gulf between the technological achievements of the wealthy West and the accomplishments of the ancient cultures of Persia and elsewhere. Without the Arabic numerical system, which introduced the use of zero as a placeholder, though, the Russian plane would not have got off the ground. As Ansuman Biswas and Jem Finer say, they are putting the 'Race' back in to 'Space Race' and, as they struggle in mid-air to hold on to their carpet or stay the right way up, they perform the questionable process of image construction in the rarest of settings with a comic turn.

Biswas and Finer have worked on a number of collaborative projects since 2000. In his individual practice, Biswas has examined the nature of consciousness in poetry, performance, science, music, video and installation. Finer's work with experimental and popular music, film, photography and installation conveys an enduring fascination with deep time and space. These areas of research and practice have converged in various projects including *wave/particle* (2001), which was also developed in a microgravity environment. A box strapped to the floor of the plane contains, in one half, water, sunflower oil, glycerine and food dye; the other half is fitted with microphones and a number of Baoding balls. The resulting video triptych, although constructed through rational and highly technologised means, recalls more the atmosphere of Mark Rothko's transcendentalist paintings, the waves of liquid mutating and drifting in harmony with the sounds of the resonating metal spheres and the thrum of the aeroplane, as if inexplicably motivated or empowered to produce mesmerising beauty.

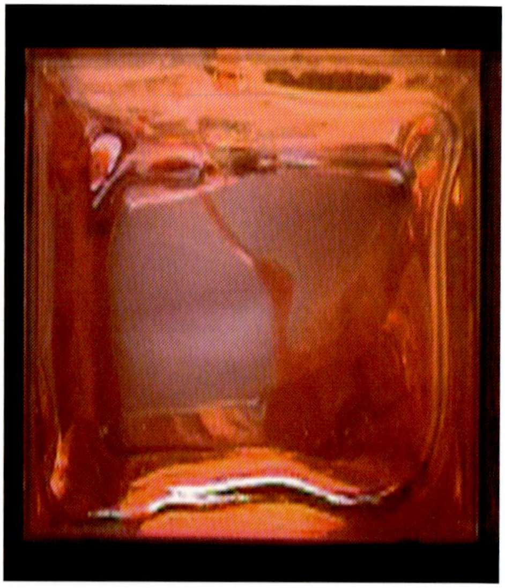

↑ *wave/particle*, 2001 (video installation, detail)
→ *Zero Genie*, 2001 (production still)

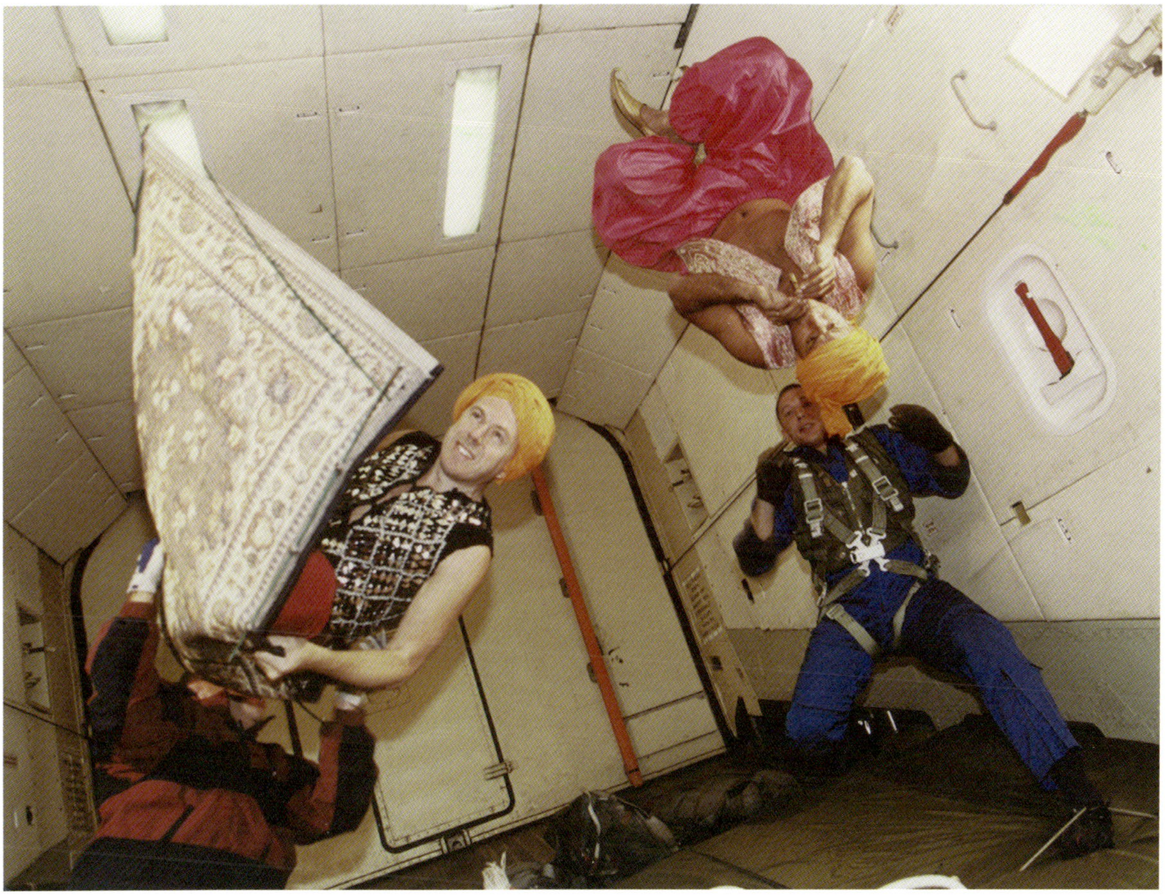

Joan Brossa

In the hands of the Catalan poet Joan Brossa (1919–98) the surrealist object becomes a device that triggers not just poetic but also political associations through its improbable coupling of diverse elements. Two lowly conjuror's wands are held aloft by an aristocratic pen stand in *Portant* [Pen Stand] (1989), while in *Sense atzar* [Without Chance] (1988), luck itself seems imprisoned, in the form of a padlocked deck of playing cards.

Brossa is best known for these small-scale sculptural works, or 'object-poems', although they are only one facet of a less recognised but proportionately larger *oeuvre* comprising poetry, prose, visual-poems, theatre works, actions, films and installations. His diverse practice developed under conditions of economic hardship and political resistance. He fought for the Second Republic in the Spanish Civil War, was co-founder in 1948 of *Dau al Set* [the seventh face of the die] – a Catalan avant-garde group that included Antoni Tàpies and Joan Ponç – and maintained a strong counter-regime position throughout the Francoist dictatorship (1939-75), which censored his work on several occasions. Set against such a life of resistance, the useless pair of scissors of *Eina Morta* [Dead Tool] (1988) seem to revolt against instituted value systems, revelling instead in the potential of an object divested of utility.

The performativity latent within Brossa's sculptural practice was described by Alexandre Cirici-Pellicer in 1972, who attended the artist's early presentation of his object-poems at Tàpies's home:

> *It should be noted that for him the form of presentation, the ritual, takes on as much importance as the physical work itself. The suspense created by the boxes which contain the objects, the mystery, the expectation of coming and going, placing each object on the table, the way of placing them and the final act, as in a variety show, of numerous presentations, all belong to his magician's world.*[1]

Brossa harboured a life-long preoccupation with stage magic and other popular performance genres. As he said in 1968, 'If I could not write, in my moments of euphoria I would be a guerrilla fighter, and in my moments of passivity, a conjuror. Being a poet includes the two things'.[2]

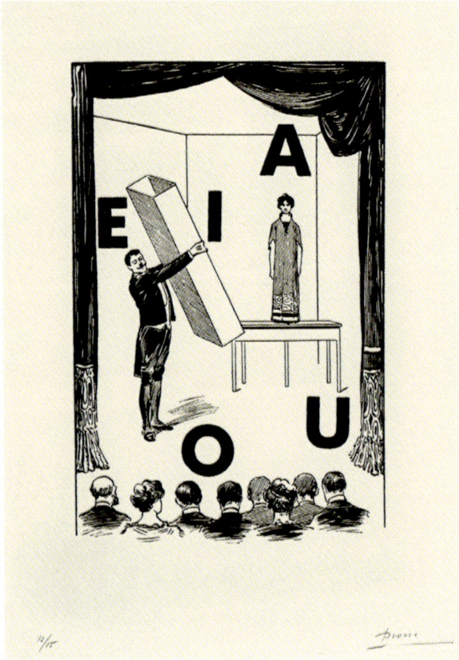

↑ *Poema visual*, 1982

→ *Sense atzar*, 1988

[1] Alexandre Cirici-Pellicer, 'La poesia visual de Joan Brossa', *Estudios Escenicos – Cuadernos de investigación teatral*, Dec. 1972. Trans. John London.

[2] Joan Brossa, *Vivàrium*, Edicions 62, Barcelona, 1972, pp. 197–98. An excerpt from an interview with A. Molina published in the newspaper *Baleares*, Palma de Mallorca, 1 Dec. 1968.

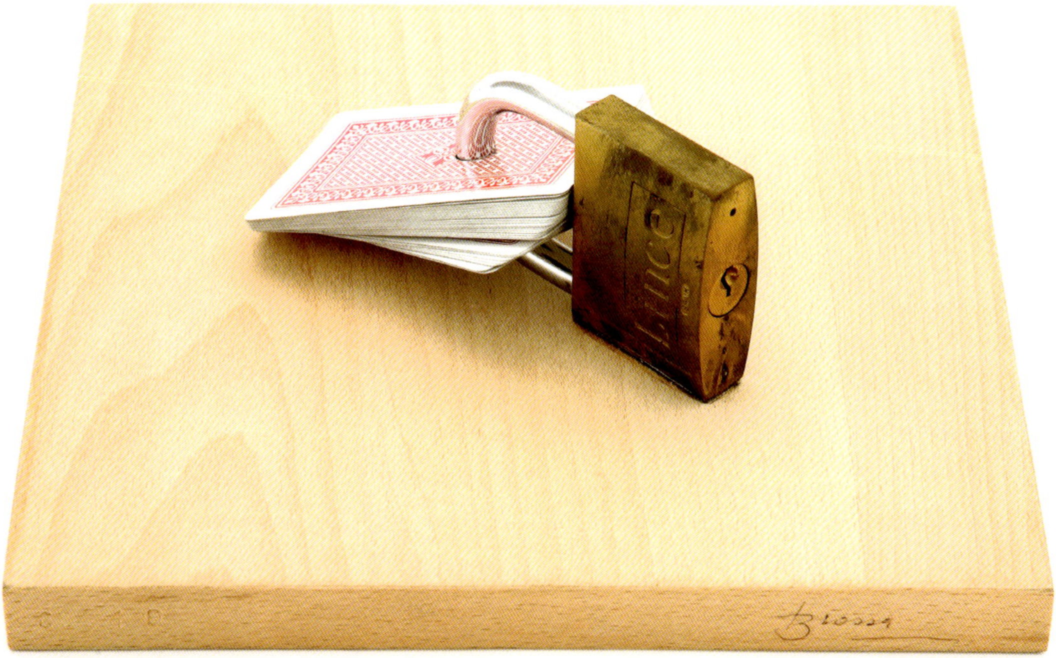

Rick Buckley

Myths and fables have long furnished humanity with the means to ritualise or scrutinise life experiences, providing tools with which to regard character and behaviour at a remove from the clouding influence of personal emotions. The collective nature of mythology, however, might be thought of as a predetermined system of speculation. What if, Rick Buckley suggests, we were to devise our own structures of belief, symbolism and interpretation?

The wall-based installation *The Incomplete Man* is a reworking of Buckley's book of the same name, which takes the reader on a metaphysical journey through an ever-evolving world of signification and surrealism. The voyage opens with a declaration of intent, demanding forward thinking, decisive action and the shrugging off of received logic:

Come my fellow conscious spirit,
Take up arms and march forth
Upon the domain of apathy & regression
Keep thy eyes focused towards the future.
Free thyself from the shackles
of thy rectrodiction.
The past has its usage for the poet,
But he must render himself to the cause
of the visionary.

Throughout, internal demons and melancholic musings are brought into view through these personal myths, with psychology manifest as magical signifiers. The protagonist, a miner plumbing the dark depths of the subconscious, seeks truth among the 'facets of reason' but finds only vapour escaping from the 'arsehole of the earth'. Parallel quests – for the source of melancholy or traces of the phantoms of loss – crisscross the miner's path. Although partly illuminated by the lucidity of geometry, the expedition ultimately falters in the shadows of the past.

The imagery that provides the mode of transport for much of this journey has been accumulated from varied sources, from archeology to film to the artist's own drawings. They convey a criticism of contemporary society's tendency to create cults through arbitrary but ultimately hidden constructs. As Buckley puts it, culture is 'like a magician's conjuring act, which denies its viewer access to its mechanism, wherein the seduction of the object draws its prey into a state of intoxication'.

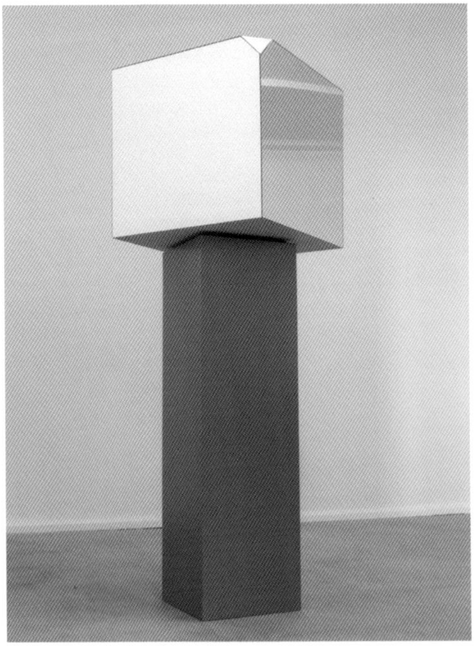

↑ *Monument*, 2008
→ *Cult #1*, 2008

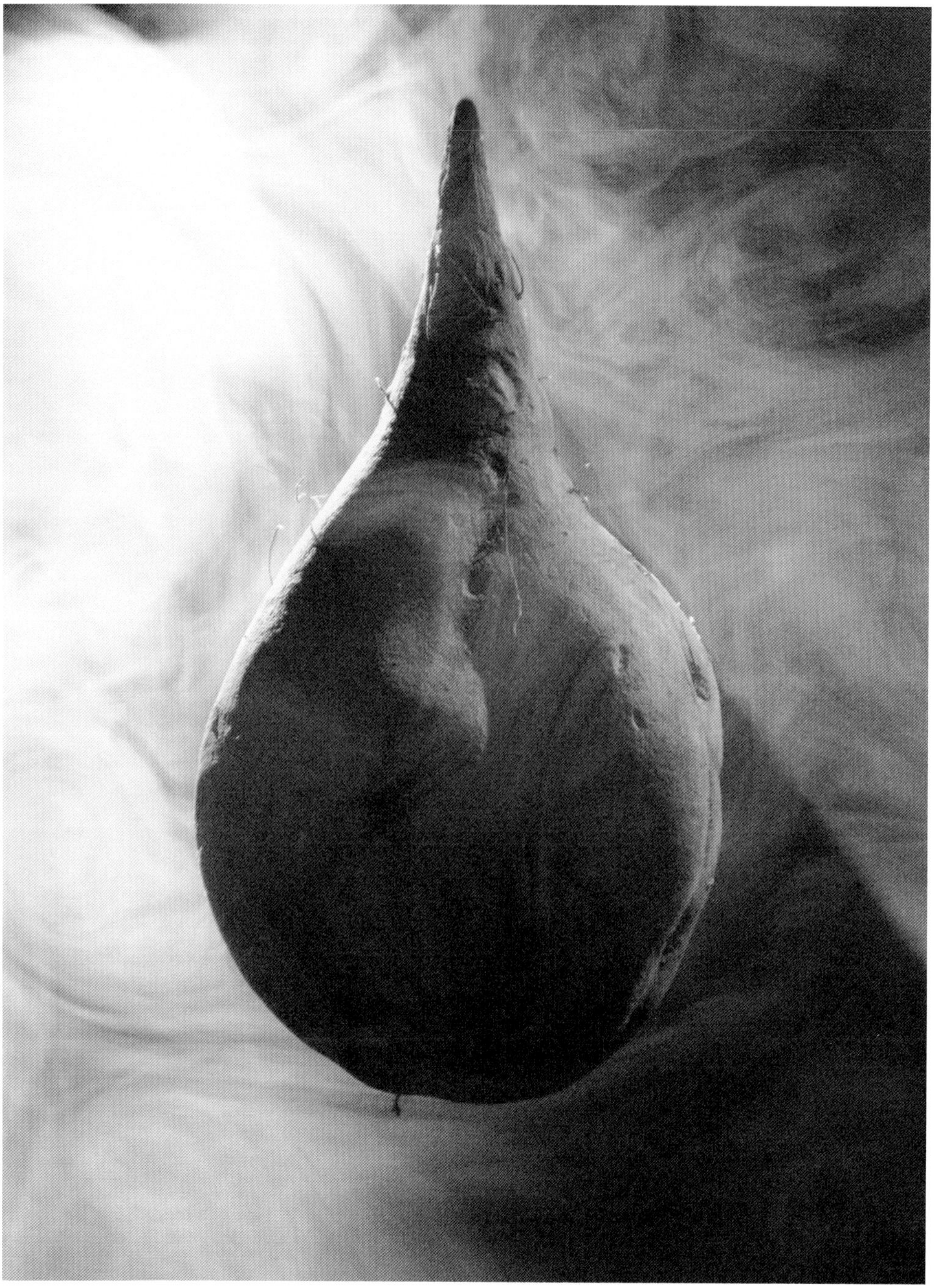

Brian Catling

ALTHOUGH Brian Catling's output has shuttled between performance, sculpture, film, video and poetry, he has been consistently preoccupied with arcane ritualism and the evocative ambiguity of image, object and language. His *Notes and Bones from a Conjuror's Table* (2009) is a tabletop assemblage that appears to fall between a collation of apparatus and artefacts, of objects of intention and evidence. A jawbone and a mechanised rib cage might be reconstructions or propositions, depending on whether we are looking at a correspondence with invention or autopsy. The materials from which they are wrought are suitably redolent, too, of prosthetics and medical models, made to look as close to the biological as possible, while promoting the clean workings of technology.

Within the micro-landscape of *Notes and Bones* small mechanical events occur at intervals, as if elements of life itself were being configured in prototype. The scene reminds us of the gothic laboratory, where animism is brewed in a crucible, as well as the wipe-clean lab of today, where the invisible phenomena of genetics and neurology are researched and instrumentalised. For Catling, the histories of technology, mythology and hermetic esoterica are ineluctable: although one era overturns the beliefs of another, this does not diminish the impact of debunked beliefs on the previous, complicit society.

Catling's performing personae range from the comic puppeteer to the sinister cabalist. His form is at once imposing and elusive, as he applies equivalent strategies of recognisability, obsolescence and invention to his costumes and actions. In his performative installation *Antix* (2005), from which the ribcage of *Notes and Bones* has been derived, the setting – part courtroom, part pulpit, part interactive technology display – becomes the lair of a menacing mute who manipulates his props to unknowable ends and abducts the occasional audience member, vanishing them to the bowels of the installation. While art-historical references to the shamanism of Joseph Beuys abound, it is perhaps more the rich history of humankind's quest for knowledge and power through induction and deduction that infuses Catling's work. From runes to dowsing to keyhole surgery, the instrumental figments of the creative imagination continue to bewitch, perhaps especially when they are unmoored from the scene of their practical application.

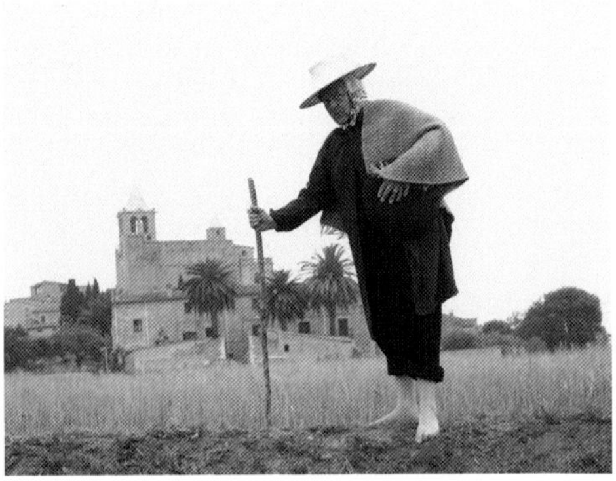

↑ *Madremanya Magi*, 2009

→ *Notes & Bones from a Conjuror's Table*, 2009 (working sketch)

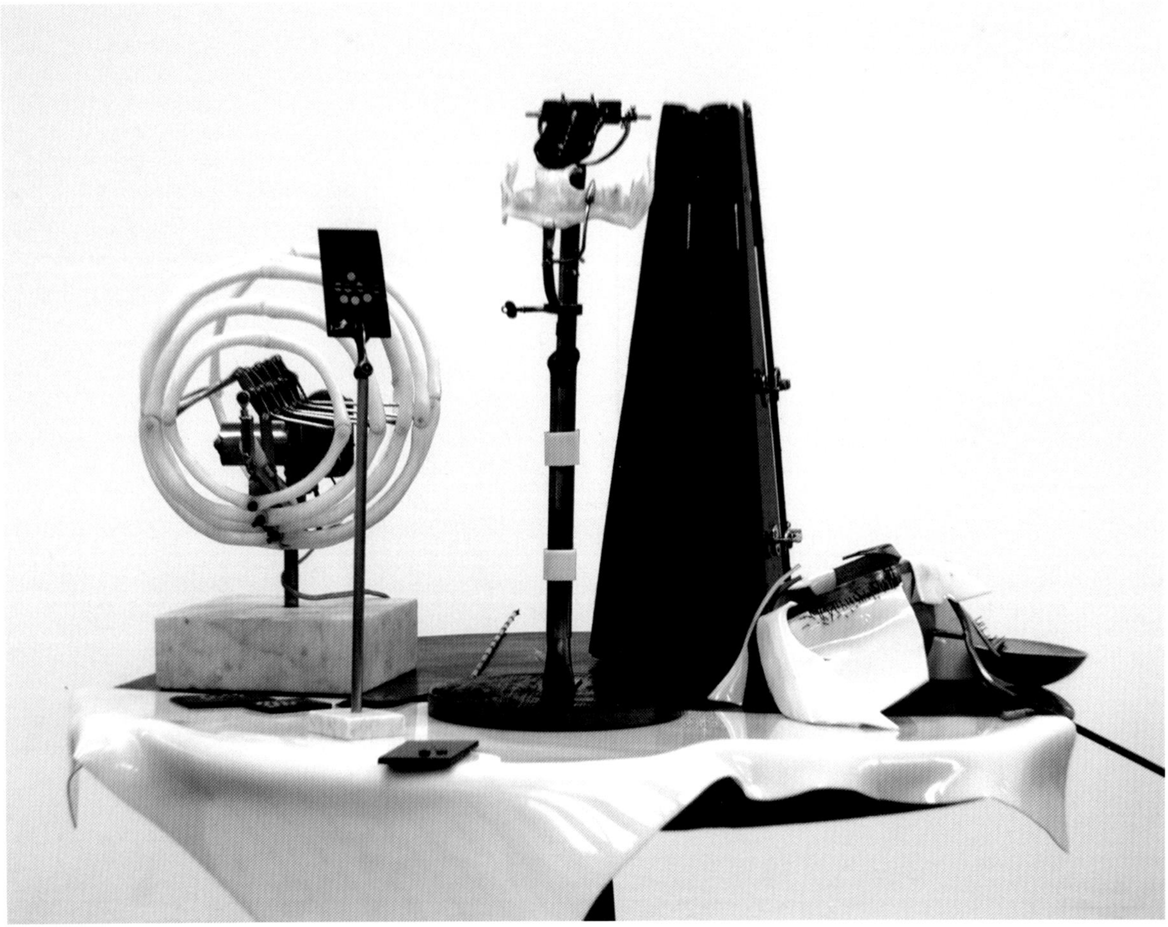

Center for Tactical Magic

THE Center for Tactical Magic integrates magical and martial practices into art in the gallery as well as in public space. Their aim is to initiate creative purposefulness that springs from an empowered multitude, intervening in an atomised society fuelled by capital-driven connoisseurship to encourage power on individual, communal and transnational fronts. These latent energies, it is hoped, can be directed toward positive social transformation. After working with private investigators, magicians and ninjas, the *Ultimate Jacket* (2003) was developed to encapsulate the processes of power dynamics common to these performers of the clandestine. The *Ultimate Jacket* has 50 pockets placed for optimum concealment and retrieval: of latex gloves for fingerprint-free passage, a balaclava to conceal identity, a low-intensity red light that enables the wearer to see without being seen or any number of other objects that enhance the wearer's agency. The jacket is made from abrasion-resistant, non-reflective breathable waterproof material; fully reversible with removable sleeves, it is the perfect garment for any tactical operation, emergency situation or social occasion that requires covertness and guile.

For the Center for Tactical Magic it is important that the tropes and methods of magic are not exploited for the sake of mere spectacle. Much of their work, therefore, operates in a participatory public arena or in stealth mode, below the radar of spectacular-seeking media. Their *Smoky Hill River Outpost* (2004) is an amalgam of playhouse, pyramid, pentagon and panopticon. The multiple-level structure was a critical attempt to construct a home in a land of security where free play is potentially monitored by a bizarre array of technologies, from wireless transmission and thumbprint scanning to astral projection and tarot.

Arthur C. Clarke recognised that 'any sufficiently advanced technology is indistinguishable from magic';[1] and indeed, in the photograph *Psychic Surveillance*, extra-sensory and electrosensory perceptions – the crystal ball and the liquid crystal display – collide head-on. Surveillance, the image suggests, is simply the contemporary manifestation of an ancient desire to perceive and control the hidden forces of the universe. The major difference is, perhaps, that surveillance culture identifies humanity, rather than demons or ghosts, as the enemy to be guarded against.

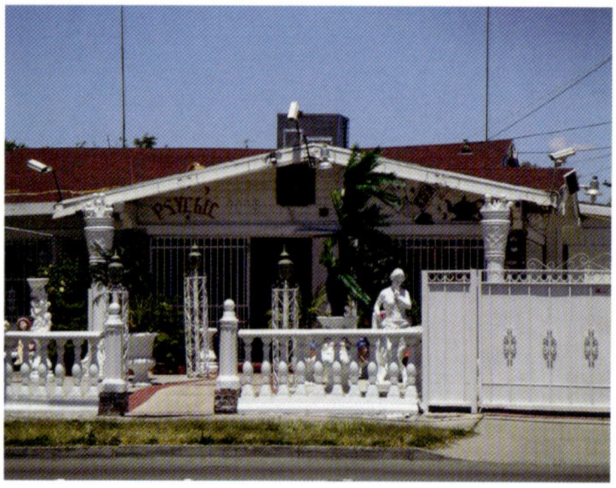

↑ *Psychic Surveillance*, 2009

→ *Ultimate Jacket (Action Poster)*, 2003

[1] Arthur C. Clarke, 'Hazards of Prophecy: The Failure of the Imagination', *Profiles of the Future*, Harper & Row, New York, 1962, p. 21.

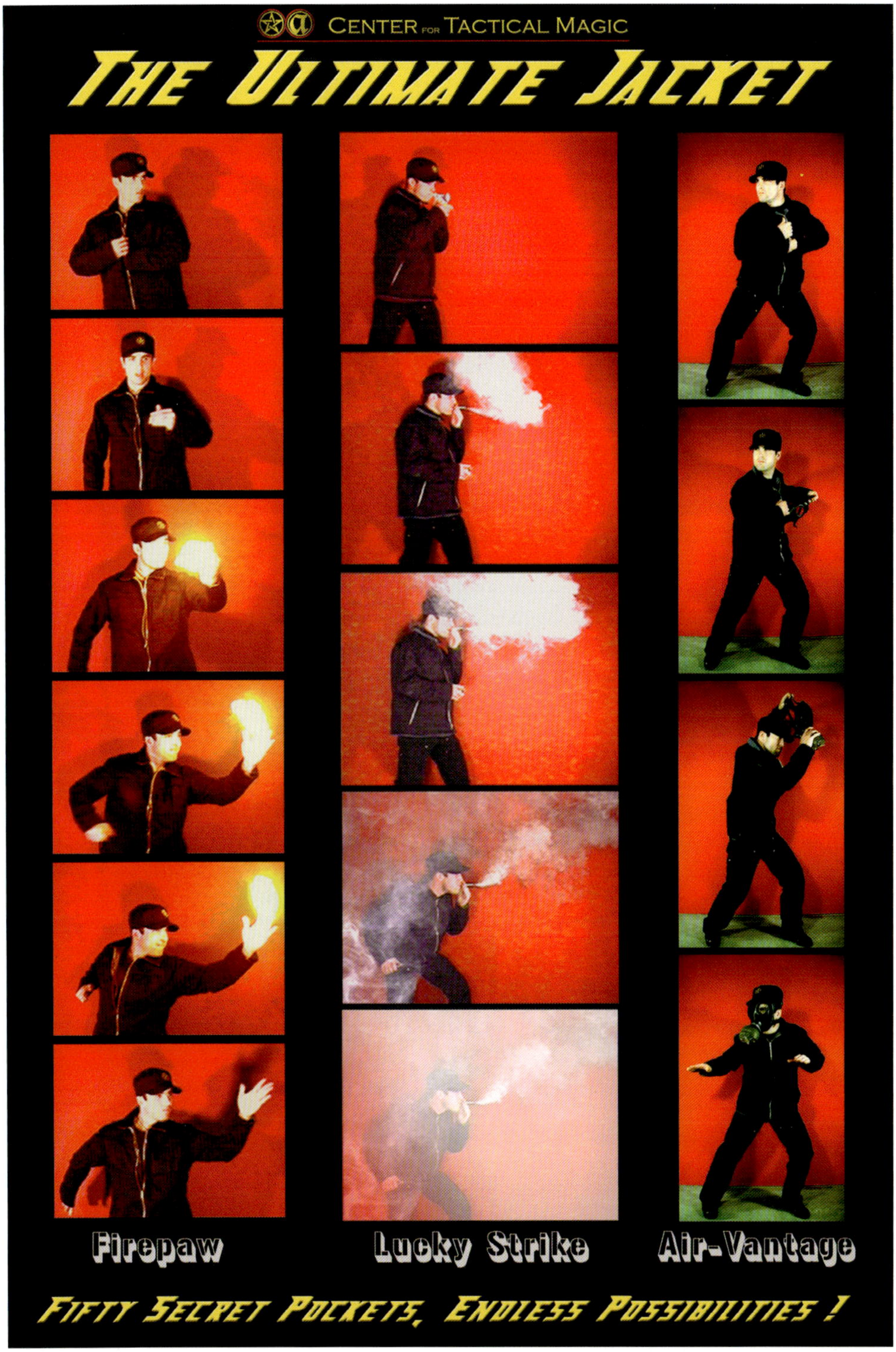
CENTER FOR TACTICAL MAGIC
THE ULTIMATE JACKET
Firepaw
Lucky Strike
Air-Vantage
FIFTY SECRET POCKETS, ENDLESS POSSIBILITIES !

Jackie & Denise Chapwoman

JACKIE and Denise Chapwoman was the temporary *nom de guerre* of Jake and Dinos Chapman when they were going through a particularly obstreperous phase around 2001. Work made during this period follows the general ambitions for that produced by their male counterparts though, in that by playing the fool or prankster they draw a severe portrait of a society with seriously skewed priorities. Their painting *Arachnokitty* featured on magician Derren Brown's television programme *Trick or Treat* as part of a dramatic and emotively charged mentalist trick. Brown invited the art critic Adrian Searle to stab two of three identically wrapped canvases, one of which was a real Chapwomans' painting, bearing a significant price tag. Following the successful performance of the trick, in which the real painting was astonishingly unscathed, the artists goaded Searle into stabbing the now revealed *Arachnokitty* just for the sake of it, which the critic, after protestation and prevarication, did with a mixture of relish and horror.

Using the vehicle of the television studio to amplify a sense of theatre, the artists, like Brown, encouraged Searle's latent desire to perform. The slashed canvas represents a moment of transgression that was previously fabricated through playful illusion in the hands of Brown, but when carried out in actuality has all the implications of real-world concerns such as money and culpability. Similarly, in the installation *The Chapman Family Collection* (2002) the elision of McDonalds' golden arches and ethnographic and reliquary fetish objects holds a mirror up to our value systems and blindspots. The installation suggests a parity between 'blind faith' in pantheistic or shamanic gods of primitive cultures, and the pervasion of cultural pillaging and corporate colonialism within developed, post-industrial societies.

The Chapman brothers repeatedly show disregard for authority, authorship and veneration of form. The latter extends not only to a patricidal approach to image making, by 'vandalising' Goya prints, for instance, but also to a grotesque take on the human body. Their obscenely mutated mannequins embody categorical chaos, where genetic engineering and social niceties are out of sync, and where mutilation arises out of the very conditions that humankind creates. *Arachnokitty*, then, signifies an instance of 'vandalism' brought about by the bourgeois spectacle of both the theatrical magic show and the rampant art market.

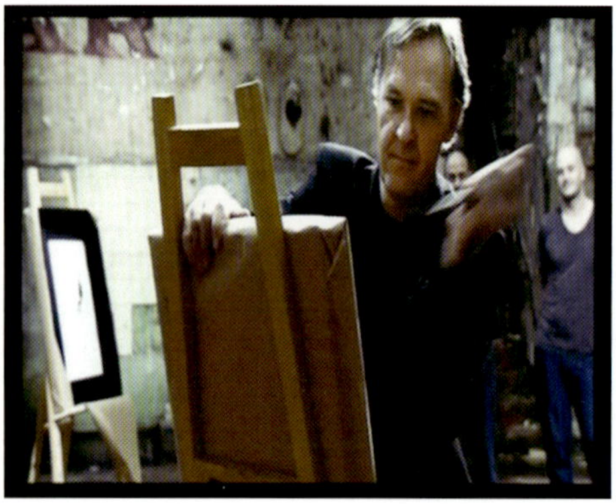

↑ Episode of Derren Brown's *Trick or Treat* featuring Jake and Dinos Chapman and Adrian Searle

→ *When Art Critics Go Bad (Arachnokitty)*, 2001/2006

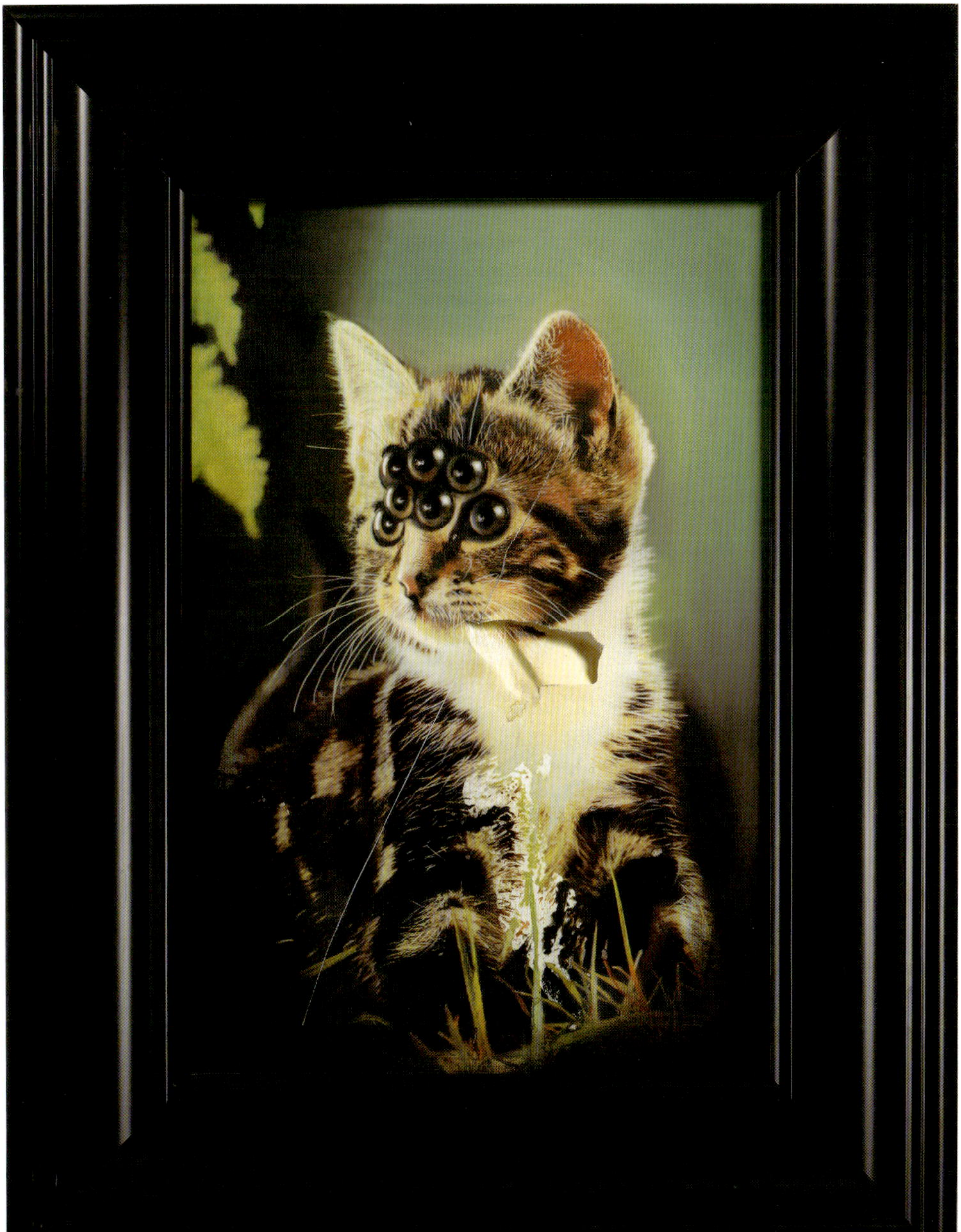

Tom Friedman

A WHITE plinth, that perennial elevator of an object to the status of art, here is literally imbued with an aura of potency. Tom Friedman confers the status of art on to the plinth entirely through the title, *Untitled (A Curse), an eleven-inch spherical space eleven inches above a pedestal cursed by a witch* (1992), in which a number of signifying strata can be identified. The 'Untitled' element locates us in the art-historically comfortable realm of codified image making, where the lack of title signals an insistence on ambiguity and, by extension, subjective interpretation by each viewer – a standard conceptual stance of artists and critics since the 1960s. The word 'curse', on the other hand, is a much more problematic signpost by which the artist baits our credulity. Artists are generally viewed by society at large as occupying an ethically considered position and, while criticism and exposé of institutional structures has been accepted as part of the artist's role in countering orthodoxy, lying is perhaps seen as rather too close to the methodology of the more powerful structures for comfort.

By cursing – or at least pretending to have cursed – a sphere of air, Friedman acknowledges the vestiges of magical thinking that still generate a double-take in sophisticates of the current era. Although causality and synchronicity could traditionally be dressed up as curses or hexes by those claiming control over invisible forces, these days such 'supernatural events' can be drummed up through illusion by those with knowledge of disciplines such as psychology and behavioural analysis. Likewise, the theatrical mindreader, or mentalist, is likely to achieve effects through subliminal direction or simple body language techniques, just as the artist considers how an image is looked at as much as how it appears. But Friedman is more interested in the mild shock of cognitive disorientation than in evoking an omnipotent figure of transformative influence, and it is the power to re-imagine in us all that he goads. He transmogrifies the banal, the unassuming or the mildly taboo into a fabulous creature or a form that evidences an equally mythical process of intense labour. From a carved aspirin to a sheet of paper that has been stared at for 1000 hours to scores of dollar bills cut into strips and repatriated into a fuzzy, expanded version, Friedman's artworks are talismans of the artist's labour and the viewer's credulity.

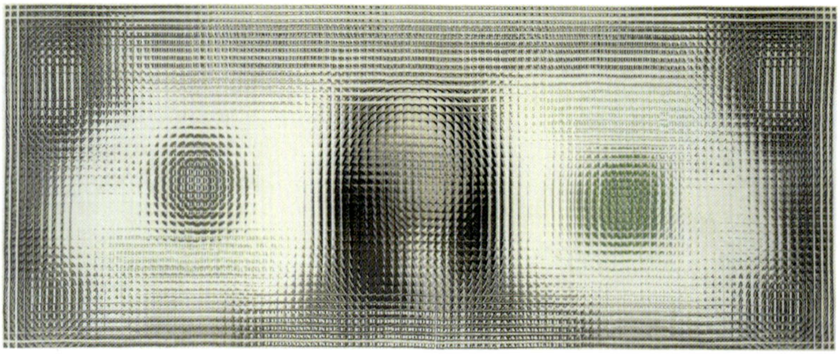

↑ *Untitled (Dollar Print)*, 2000

→ *Untitled (A Curse), an eleven-inch spherical space eleven inches above a pedestal cursed by a witch*, 1992

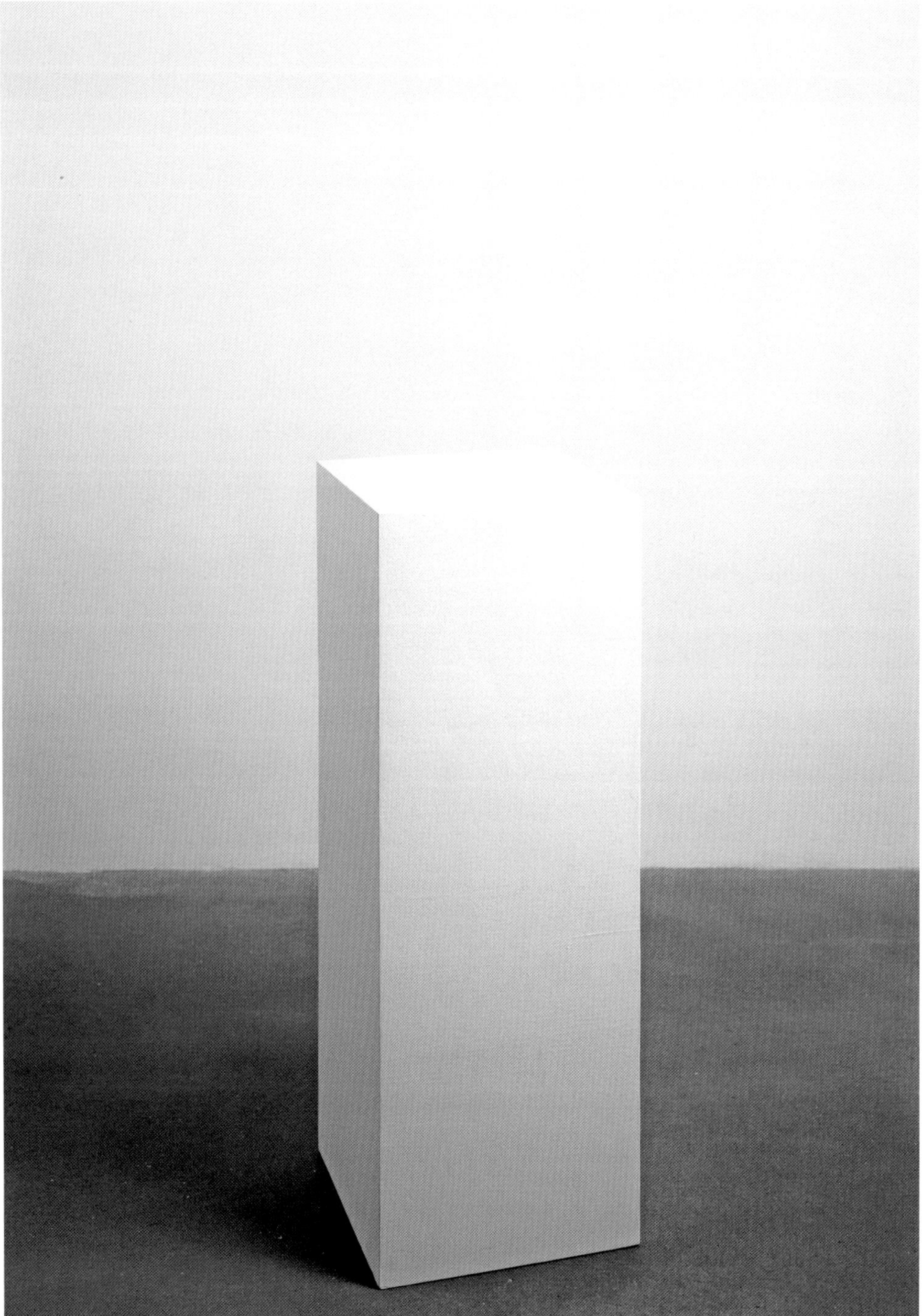

Brian Griffiths

A PIECE of furniture wrenched from its life of utility seems stranded in the gallery as if awaiting reassignment. Approach with curiosity, though, and a pair of feet become visible at its base, while at eye level a pair of peepholes reveals the distinct absence of a body. *Daylight Ned* (2007), Brian Griffiths's partial-vanishing cabinet, is a mechanism of wonderment that does not present an all-singing, all-dancing act of marvel, but rather produces a gently creeping sense of potential.

Griffiths's materials originate in the banal world of domesticity: the wardrobes favoured by bed-sit landlords, utilitarian waterproof clothing, modestly priced vintage statuettes, wooden mantelpiece-dwelling antelopes. They speak of humble aspirations, decorative embellishment and status-claiming, albeit of a mundane order that misses the higher hallmarks. The objects and images they are transformed into, however, articulate fantasies of an altogether different register. *Daylight Ned* evokes the fiction of an illusionist with the power to dematerialise. Larger gallery filling works – such as a carriage or caravan and a galleon run aground, also wrought from second-hand furniture and domestic accoutrements – promise mythical voyages through time and space on a scale beyond ordinary experience.

Griffiths chases down archetypal figures and situations such as the pirate, the quest and the imperceptible alien, and fixes them in the stuff of the everyday. This not only elevates the overlooked through the agency of imagination, but also reveals how we project narration and anthropomorphism on to inert matter. It is impossible, suggests Griffiths, to contemplate two objects placed together – a rabbit and a horn, perhaps – without generating an internal logic, no matter how absurd. The sculptor, like the magician, encourages processes of theatricalisation through contiguity, diverting and converting our usual patterns of thought. But whereas the magician tends to perform a disruption of logic with the goal of temporary awe, Griffiths conducts these transformations with the hope of longer-lasting contagion, permanently infecting the viewer with a compulsion to fantasise.

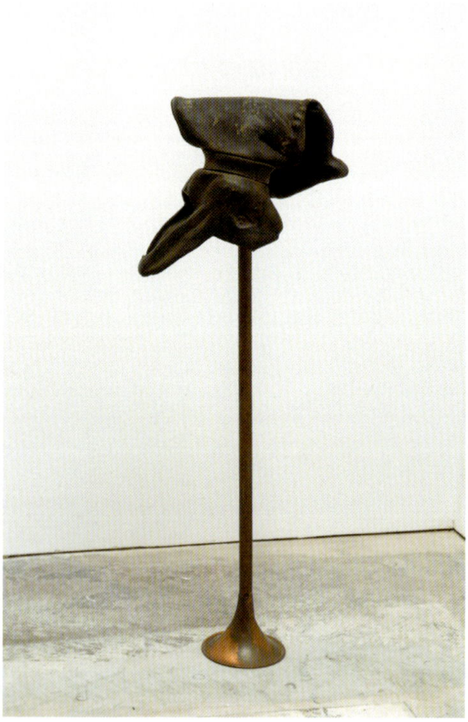

↑ *Traitor*, 2008
→ *Daylight Ned*, 2007

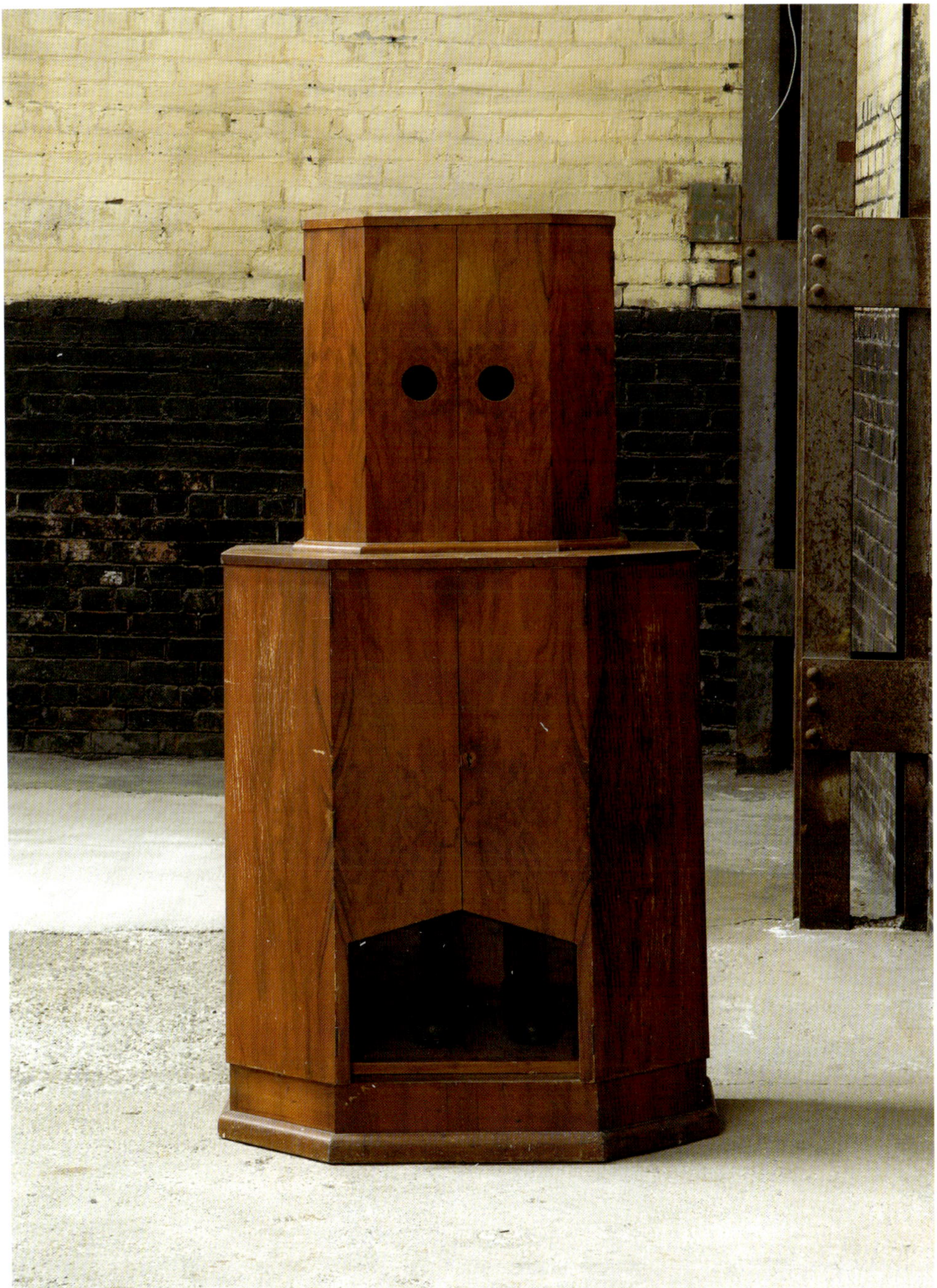

Colin Guillemet

Pairs of Polaroid photographs dotted throughout the gallery lead us on a wild goose chase of non-sequiturs. A magician's top hat with a carrot beside it evokes the traditional white rabbit that continually fails to appear. In the next pair of photographs the hat might be coupled with a parsnip, the pale cousin of the carrot, or a door wedge, whose shape slackly rhymes with a root vegetable but which brings with it a whole other world of usage and association. From image to image, we are forever one step behind – or is it ahead? – of the stock narrative triggered when we see a magician's hat and a carrot so expectantly assembled.

The inclusion of an umbrella among the carrot substitutes gives a clue to the historical precedence of Guillemet's practice, recalling Lautréamont's chance encounter of 'a sewing machine and an umbrella on an operating table'. Lautréamont's enlisting of the reader as an accomplice in the creation of fierce imagery and leaps of logic presaged the surrealists' wish to emancipate the 'madness that one locks up' as a partisan of the self-conscious adult world; and Guillemet similarly aims to overturn common sense and the very idea of certainty. A sign's obedient adherence to the meaning that has been decided for it is, suggests Guillemet, an arbitrary arrangement. He is interested in what happens when disobedience is actively encouraged, when antagonistic thinking or even non-sense are ushered in. Just as structuralists might claim that knowledge is a case of tacking the right meaning to the right sign, it could be reckoned that inventiveness is learning to unhitch or rearrange this, breaking apparently fixed causal chains to invent new permutations.

While Darwin broke the chain of teleology to revelatory ends and Lewis Carroll summoned the white rabbit to enchant and amuse, the artist does so because he simply must. This compulsion to subvert the orthodox may appear a gratuitous hoax, but when Guillemet changes the colour of a canary by feeding it treated birdseed, for instance, he subverts our understanding of the meaning of 'canaryness' through a contingent somatic process steeped in chromatic beauty. Here he slakes a thirst not for the miraculous, but for the poetics of dislocation and, like magic and technology, offers a glimpse of human power over the apparently inevitable.

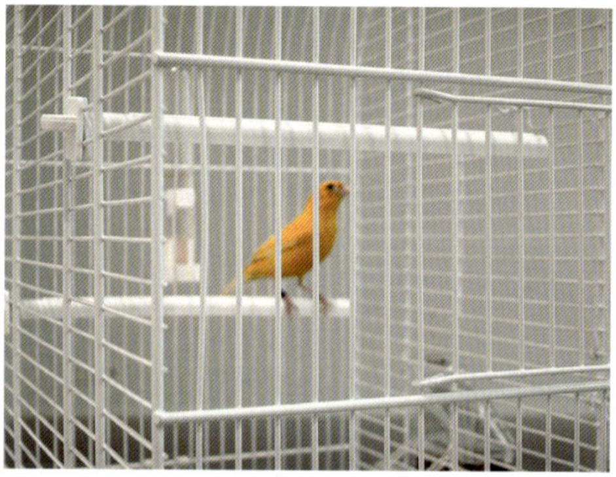

↑ *Canary Shift*, 2005
→ *Untitled (anything but a rabbit)*, 2006 (detail)

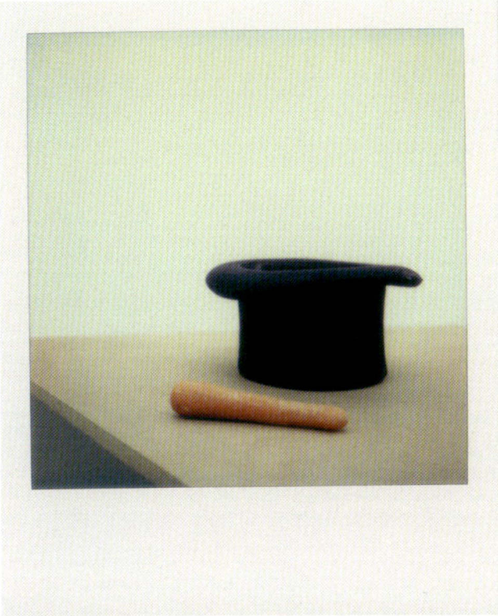

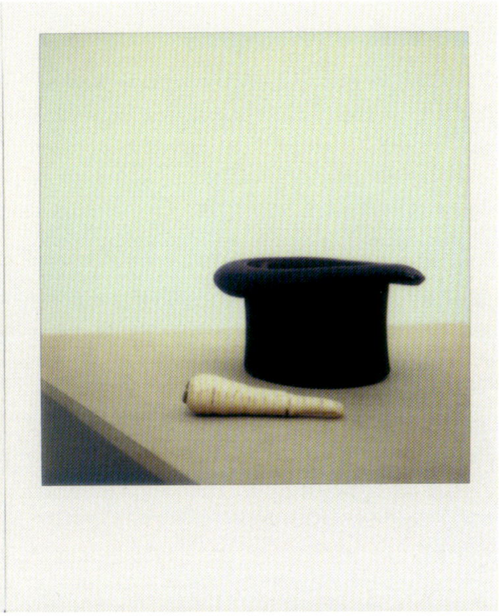

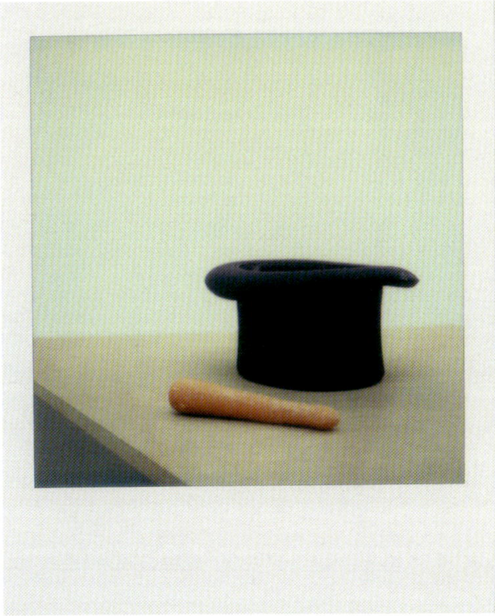

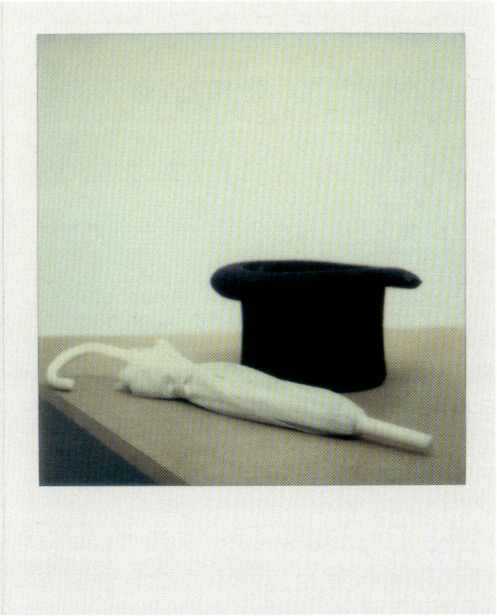

João Maria Gusmão & Pedro Paiva

THE phrase 'unnatural order' seems to pervade João Maria Gusmão & Pedro Paiva's silent 16mm films as a mantra-like edict. Trees, rocks, water, rope and bones behave anomalously, abandoning the rational rehearsal of laws of gravitational pull, entropy or inanimate inertia and cleaving instead to a different narrative where anticipation, tension and resolution roll out with poetic succinctness. While the films' tight frame of focus, regarding each event with cool detachment, seems more analytical than emotive, the empirical evidence we witness owes more to the literary imagination than to scientific findings.

In this selection of films, which barely scratches the surface of Gusmão & Paiva's output, physicality is drenched in metaphysical import. The relationship between human protagonist – whether in the frame or apparent through the ropes or cranes that they make little effort to hide – and the world of objects with which they interact verges on magical realism, as unknowable meaning and untenable power are embedded in simple nonsensical developments. A falling tree, rolling stones and a skeleton growing antlers are distended with symbolism that is divorced from its originating event or circumstance.

Many of the films are shot in ambiguous landscapes verging on desert or scrubland, while representations of human habitats often have an ethnographic accent, recalling anthropological films of the early 20th century. The strategic placing of these events beyond the everyday backdrop of Western European society heightens our sense of expectation and encourages certain archetypal projections and assumptions about non-secular societies. In a similar tactic, Gusmão & Paiva use the now near-obsolete technology of 16mm to call upon the theatrical qualities of early cinema, rather than simply revelling in its nostalgic and seductive aesthetic. Like the showmen of early cinema attractions, they compel their viewers through tactile and visual encounter, while the use of makeshift trickery within the films, such as cranes, ropes and editing, brings them closer to the contemporary stage magician. And yet this calculated divulgence of mechanical methods only serves to create another layer of obfuscation that is more reflective of our muddled perception than our enlightened understanding.

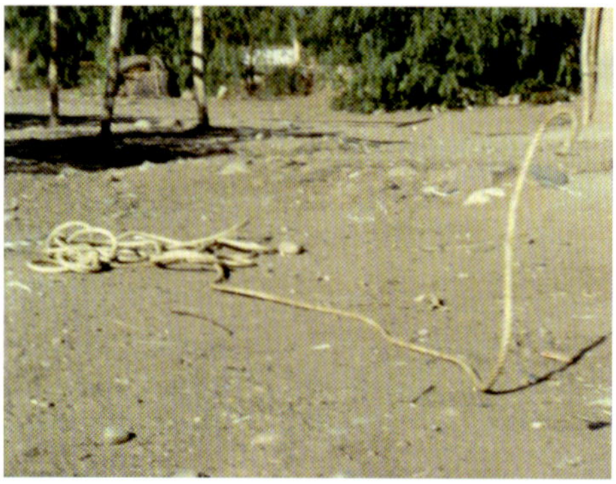

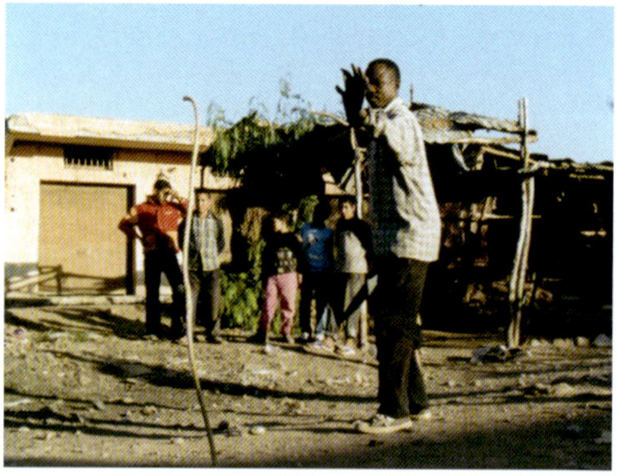

↑ *About the spirit of gravity (or the blacksmith and the cutting of the serpent)*, 2007 (video stills)

→ *Paramagnetism*, 2004 (video still)

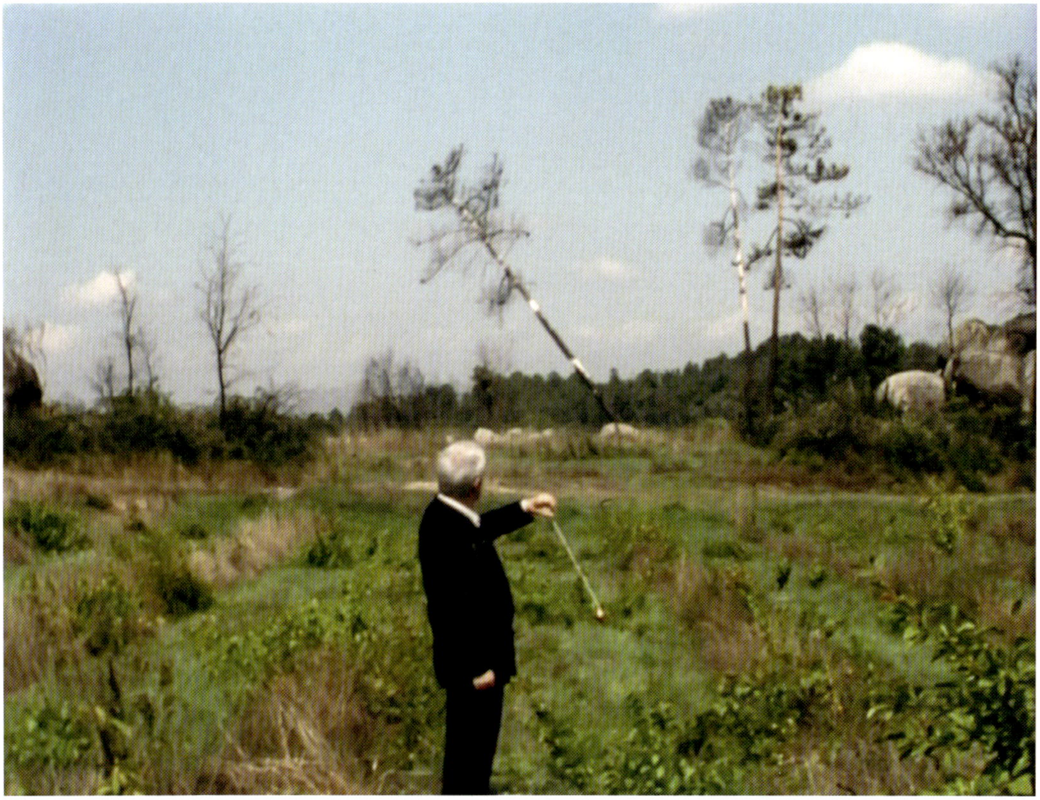

Susan Hiller

Susan Hiller's collation of images garnered from the internet depicts individuals apparently in the act of 'levitating'. In pursuit of this supernatural feat a number of strategies appear to have been employed: traditional photomontage, digital editing programmes, hydraulic machines, magnetic devices, acrobatic feats, stage illusions and time-lapse photography. Hiller's collection comprises a critical celebration of technology and the impetus that may lie behind such acts of deception. As today's sophisticated audience can instantaneously debunk the spiritualist's claims, she suggests that behind these images there is a more complex impulse expressing a collective aspiration for a revised version of humanity that is poetic, imaginative and powerful, with as-yet unrealised abilities and potentials.

The piece is also an homage to Yves Klein's iconic photograph *Leap into the Void* (1960), which was originally published with a caption explaining that the artist, 'who is also a judo champion, black belt, 4th Dan, trains regularly in dynamic levitation (with or without a net!), at risk to his life.' In fact, Klein jumped from a ledge about 15 feet high and asked a dozen or so judo friends to hold a tarpaulin to catch his fall. The final image is a montage, the original fake.

Hiller considers Klein's photograph part of a long-established tendency in modernist art to make use of certain mystical or spiritual traditions derided as superstitious by scientific rationalism. Throughout her practice she has paid close attention to the social and cultural implications of this collision, blending art and science, poetry and analysis, the sensual and the investigative. An early project, *Dream Mapping* (1974), for instance, involved a number of participants working together to devise a system of diagrams to describe their dreams, the universalising scientific language of graphic notation made poetically absurd in the light of the subject matter. Likewise, *Magic Lantern* (1987) presents archival audio recordings collected by 'ghost-hunters' alongside hard-edged technology that projects simple circles of coloured light. While the ghostly sounds pique the imagination, the light installation affects the body. The hues that play on the retina generate unknowable depths of experience and associations, and external reality and internal perception are thrown once more into unsteady relation.

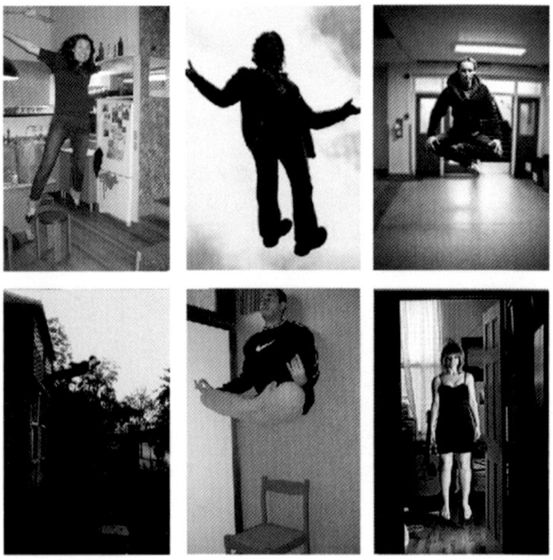

↑ *Homage to Yves Klein*, 2008 (detail)

→ *Homage to Yves Klein*, 2008

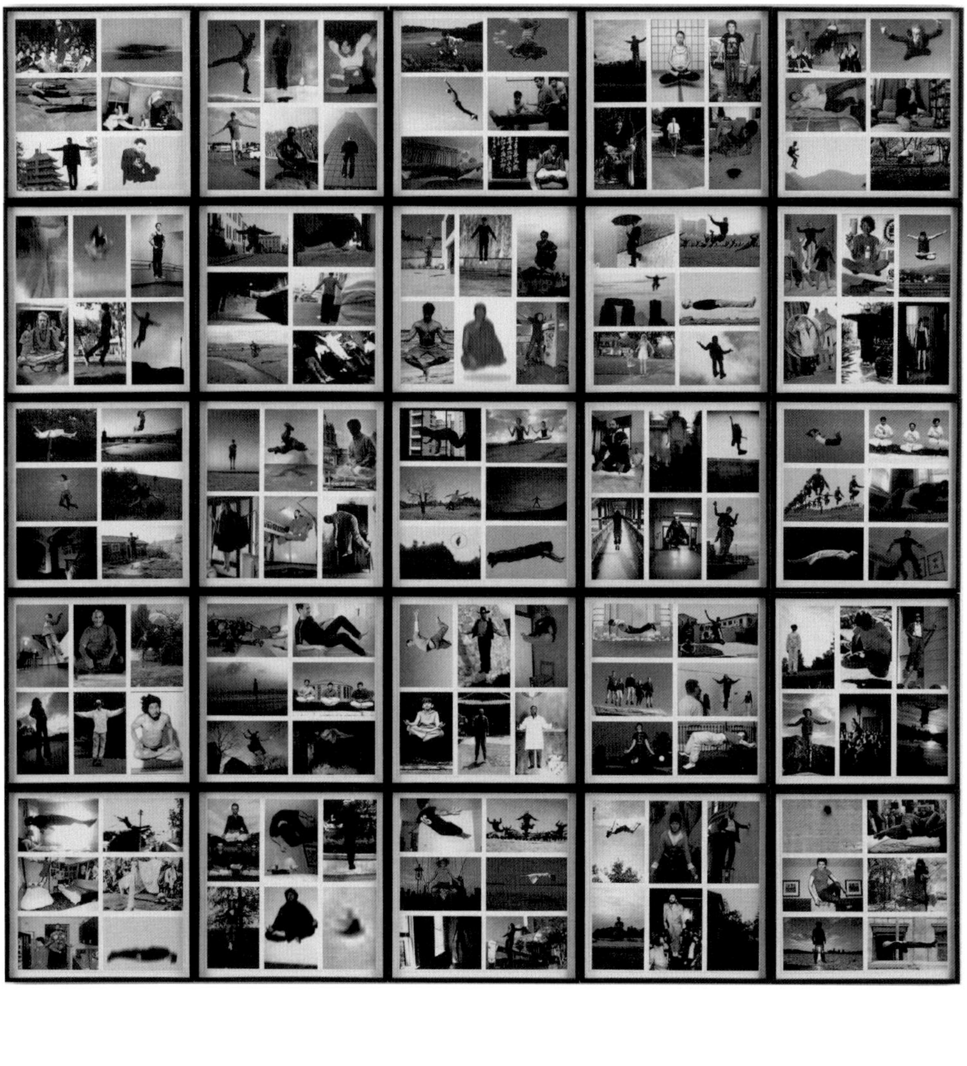

Alexandra Hopf

ALEXANDRA Hopf's *Gehülfen* (2008) are named after the figures that, as Walter Benjamin noted, appear throughout Franz Kafka's stories.[1] An old German word for helpmates or assistants, *Gehülfen* may be both obstructive and obliging, interposing between the realm of the known and the mysterious. They appear when we are paying least attention, causing us to stumble, or disappearing vital items from our pockets. Benjamin characterised them as creatures originating in a pre-linguistic era, a symptom of a repressed atavism made visible as a nervous tic. We might also think of them as tricksters operating between layers of perception and visualisation, which Hopf accentuates through a mask-like mien that is at once theatrical and melancholic, like an apparition caught on camera, eager to speak but ultimately voiceless.

The images are made by spraying fine layers of paint on to the back of sheet glass. In this way, the painting is built up in reverse, with the background applied last and the initial gestures blurred by the process of finessing. Hopf often works from pre-existing imagery, absorbing other authors into a visual vocabulary that is at once referential and self-referential, with source material compressed through the process into a single, seductive surface. At times the artist's associations are revealed, at others their origin is mysteriously obscured so that, like history itself, imagery is experienced as part illusion, part projection.

Often the works are hung in idiosyncratic arrangements that recall cabinets of curiosities, where scientific knowledge is inflected by a previous superstitious era. *The Destiny Maschine* (2009), for instance, draws on Surrealist modes of display formulated by designer Friedrich Kiesler (1896–1965), recruiting them as an allegory for contemporary display, artifice and the generation of desire. As Hopf describes, the work invites us 'to throw a glance at a deception through the window pane, in the awareness that this gaze is being returned as an iridescent camouflage'.

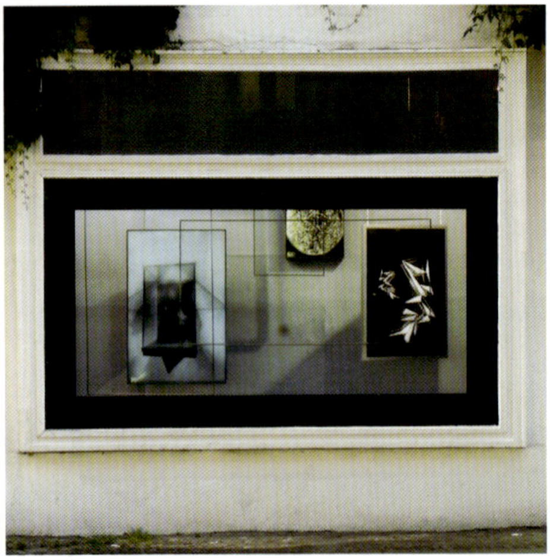

↑ *The Destiny Maschine*, 2009

→ *Gehülfe D (Assistant D)*, 2008

[1] Walter Benjamin, 'Franz Kafka', *Illuminations*, Pimlico, London, 1999, pp. 108–135.

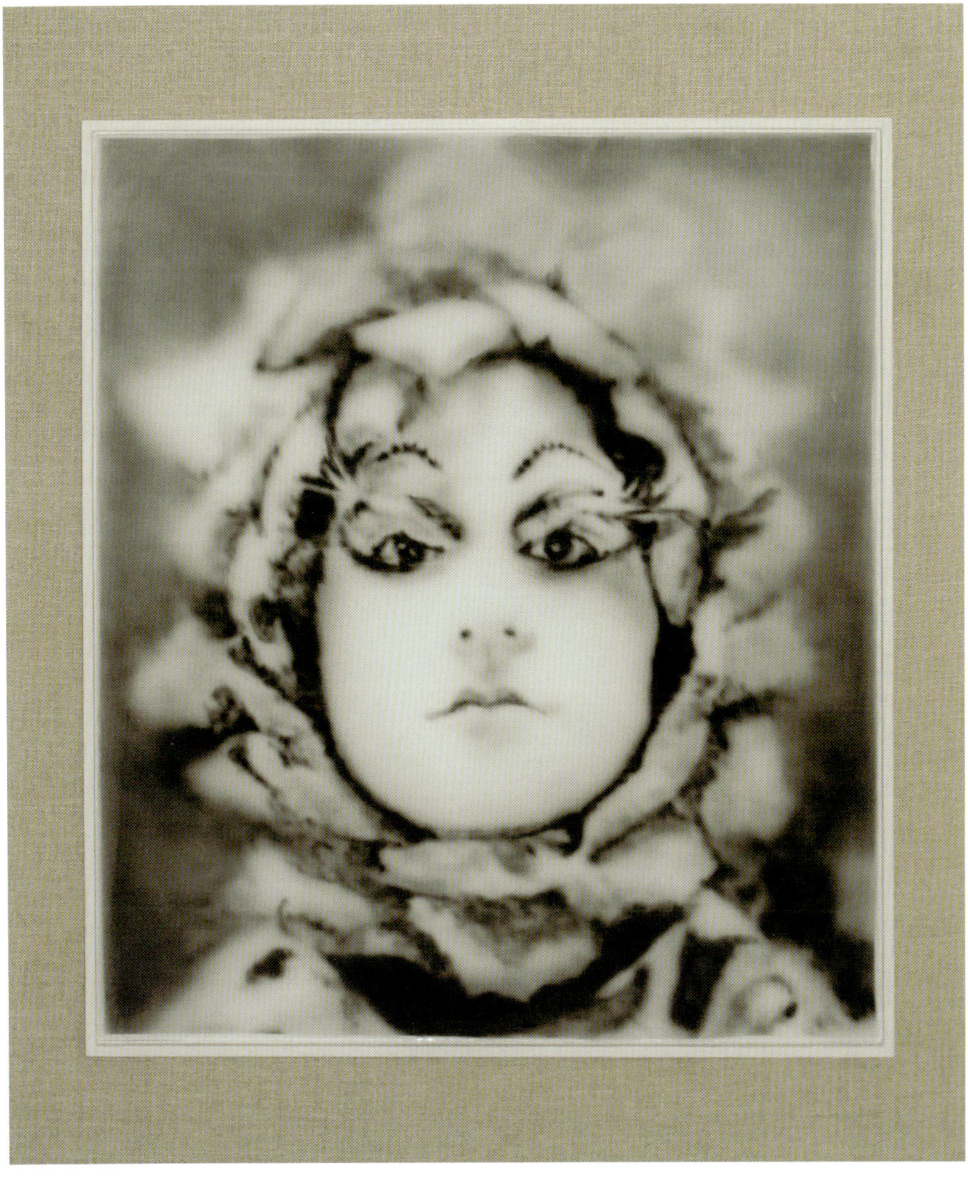

Christian Jankowski

CHRISTIAN Jankowski deploys tricksterish tactics to cast a spotlight on the oddities and artifice of special-interest nooks of the commercialised world. In *Telemistica*, a piece commissioned for the 48th Venice Biennale, he turns his attention to the high-grossing industry of television call-ins, phoning five cable TV fortune tellers from his hotel room and asking them live on air for their predictions on the future success of the artwork he was currently developing. Unwittingly, the fortune tellers' own pronouncements – which are, needless to say, unremittingly upbeat – not only constitute a prophecy on the reception of the work, but also its content – a curiously paradoxical situation that demonstrates the self-transforming potential of the tactical artist's scenarios.

Jankowski regularly works with collaborators of varying levels of self-awareness and compliance, playfully mirroring their modes and mores back to them. He has invited horror-movie convention-goers to deliver a threat, in full gory costume, to the person on whom they would most like to be avenged; collaborated with an evangelist pastor to deliver a sermon on art; facilitated the ascendance of a Greek television talkshow to the status of artwork, and chaired a puppet conference where such luminaries as Fozzy Bear and Lamb Chop were invited to describe their art and their relationship with television. In each instance, Jankowski obliges those who are used to presenting an illusory narrative through genre conventions to show the creaking mechanisms and clichés that lie behind them. In a way, then, his strategy resembles the debunking magician who, once he has revealed how another magician's tricks are performed, goes on to bamboozle with yet another layer of illusion – in this case, the artwork itself.

This is complicated further in Jankowski's *Magic Circle* trilogy (1998–2002), where the artist cedes creative authority to a sequence of magicians who turn him into a dove, a gallery director into a poodle and an exhibition audience into sheep. While we know that the stage magician dupes us and the editing process further leads our perception, we nonetheless remain beguiled. The mystery becomes not how the trick is performed, but how its effect is sustained – no matter how enlightened we are as to its cause.

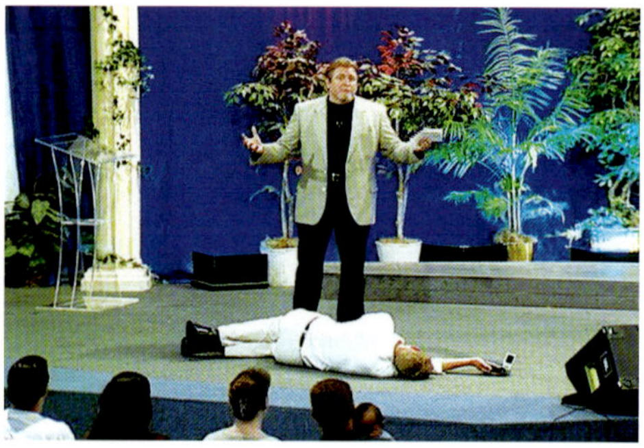

↑ *The Holy Artwork*, 2001 (video still)
→ *Telemistica*, 1999 (video stills)

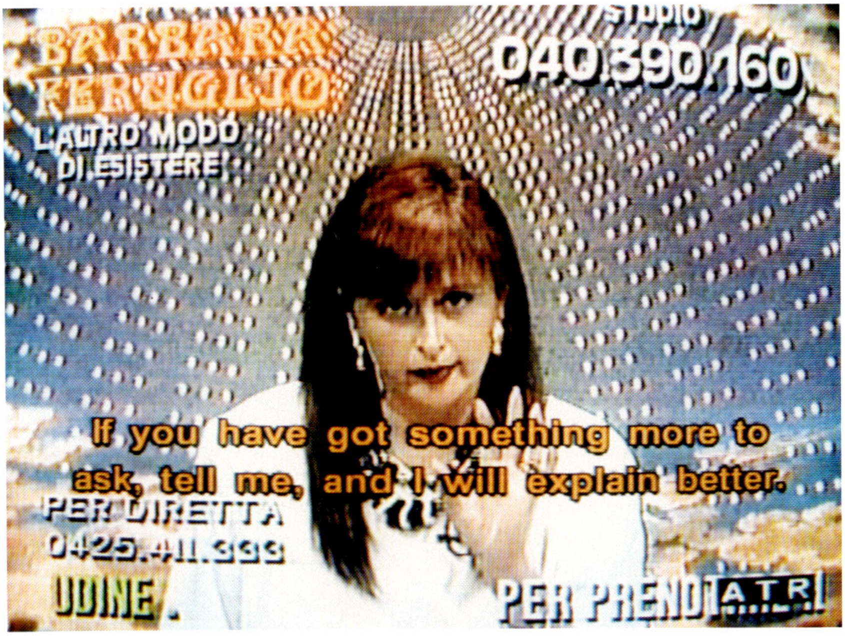
BARBARA FERUGLIO
040 390 160
L'ALTRO MODO DI ESISTERE!
If you have got something more to ask, tell me, and I will explain better.
PER DIRETTA
0425.411.333
UDINE .
PER PRENOTARE
A.T.R.

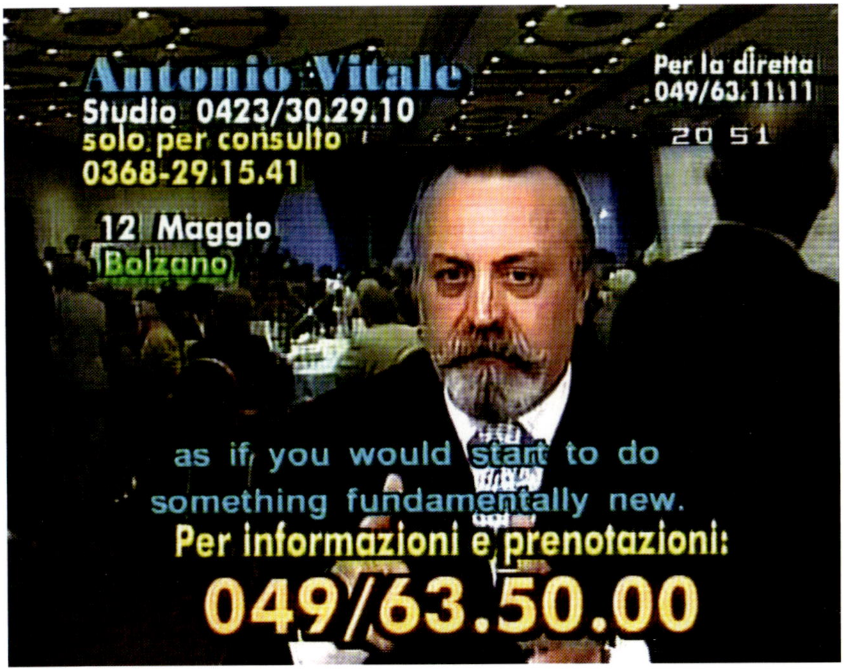
Antonio Vitale
Studio 0423/30.29.10
solo per consulto
0368-29.15.41
Per la diretta
049/63.11.11
20 51
12 Maggio
Bolzano
as if you would start to do something fundamentally new.
Per informazioni e prenotazioni:
049/63.50.00

Janice Kerbel

Janice Kerbel's *Home Conjuring Unit* (2000) presents itself as a set of assembly instructions for the sort of furniture that sits overlooked in every home. In fact, these plans describe the construction of a 'Bedroom wardrobe for spontaneous appearance', a 'Storage chest for splitting in two', a 'Worktable for floating on air' and 'Nest tables for quick and easy escapes'. Each apparatus can be made from the same pieces of prepared timber so that, theoretically, the wardrobe may be converted to the nest tables and the nest tables into the storage chest, should the occasion require it.

Home Conjuring Unit is an apparently authoritative pattern for an absurd implausibility. This versatile piece of kit for the domestic illusionist remains forever in the imagination. As with other projects by the artist that find their eventual form as plans, maps or text pieces, the conjuring unit maintains a distance between representation and reality. In a series of posters that evoke sideshow paste-ups from days of yore, for instance, we summon wholly imagined figures: a girl whose bodily functions slow until she faints or a human firefly that spontaneously combusts. Similarly, in *Bank Job* (1999) a detailed and apparently infallible plan for the robbery of a Coutts bank in the City of London was also arrested at the planning stage, while a series of drawings of gardens suitable to very particular situations, such as in laundrettes or for council flats, although possible, are never realised.

Kerbel addresses issues of representation and power, favouring abstractions transmitted through the vagaries of subjective mental reconstruction over authoritatively concrete products. The aspirational nature of these designs and their escapist connotations imply a need for the fanciful in a world where necessity and accumulation overlap. Kerbel's series of marked playing cards, backed with a pattern that is subtly varied to indicate each card's value and suit to aid cheating by the cognisant, threaten to overstep the line between the fantastical and the instrumental. Held forever behind glass, though, they remain tantalisingly beyond reach, restoring the imbalance between idea and actual effect.

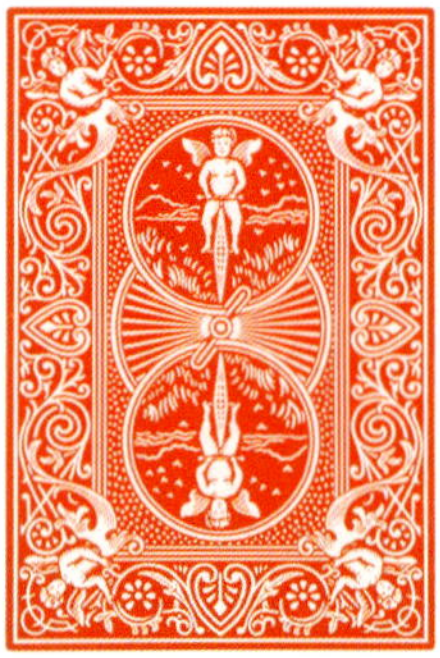

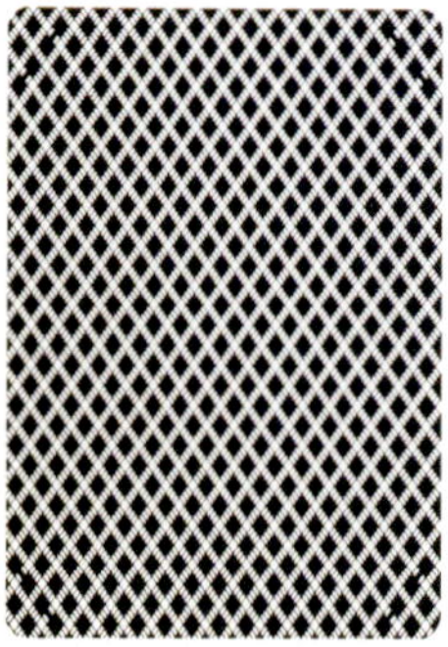

↑ *Three Marked Decks: Bicycle Riderback (poker)*, 1999 (detail); *Three Marked Decks: Bee Special Diamondback (blackjack)*, 1999 (detail)

→ *Home Conjuring Unit*, 2000

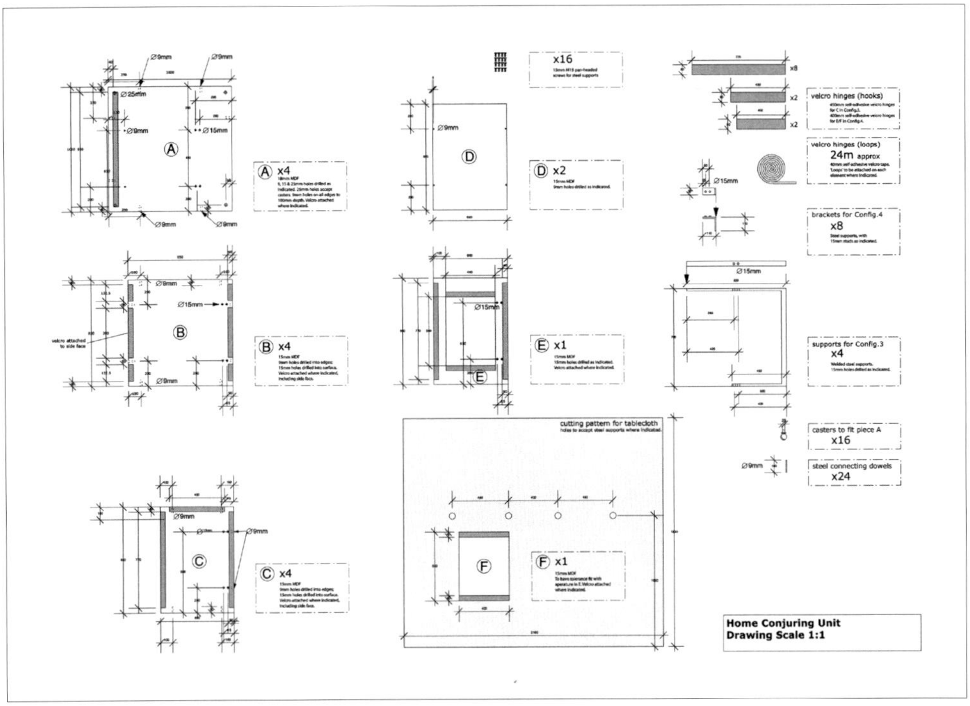

A x4
B x4
velcro attached to side face
C x4
x16
D x2
E x1
cutting pattern for tablecloth
F x1
velcro hinges (hooks)
velcro hinges (loops)
24m approx
brackets for Config.4
x8
supports for Config.3
x4
casters to fit piece A
x16
steel connecting dowels
x24
Home Conjuring Unit
Drawing Scale 1:1

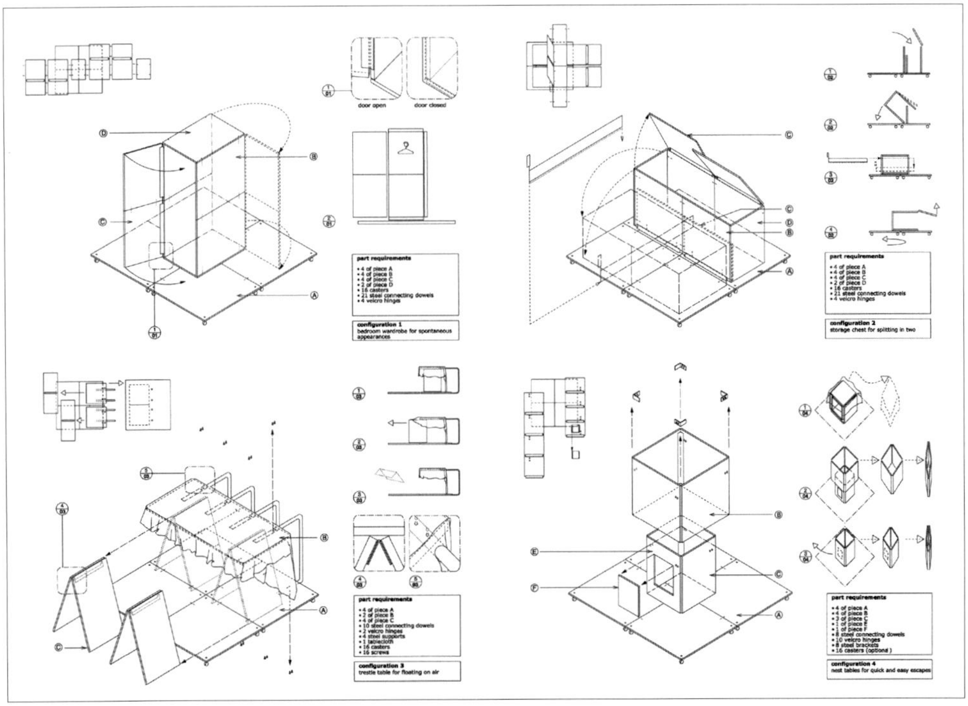

door open
door closed
part requirements
• 4 of piece A
• 4 of piece B
• 4 of piece C
• 2 of piece D
• 16 casters
• 21 steel connecting dowels
• 4 velcro hinges
configuration 1
bedroom wardrobe for spontaneous appearances
part requirements
• 4 of piece A
• 4 of piece B
• 4 of piece C
• 2 of piece D
• 16 casters
• 21 steel connecting dowels
• 4 velcro hinges
configuration 2
storage chest for splitting in two
part requirements
• 4 of piece A
• 2 of piece B
• 4 of piece C
• 10 steel connecting dowels
• 2 velcro hinges
• 4 steel supports
• 1 tablecloth
• 16 casters
• 16 screws
configuration 3
trestle table for floating on air
part requirements
• 4 of piece A
• 4 of piece B
• 3 of piece C
• 1 of piece E
• 1 of piece F
• 8 steel connecting dowels
• 10 velcro hinges
• 8 steel brackets
• 16 casters (optional)
configuration 4
nest tables for quick and easy escapes

Annika Lundgren

ANNIKA Lundgren's *Magic & Politics* (2007) is a peculiar breed of allegory that produces its symbolic power not through allusion but through literalisation. A straightforward story, simply related, tells of a conference that hosts a parade of 'trick makers' before an expectant audience. The top-billing illusionist makes a rabbit disappear, only for it to reappear offstage shortly afterwards, grab the microphone and deliver a lecture on disclosing the means behind manifestation. The rabbit and the conference translator – a woman who understands only too well that the process of transformation requires determined work, and that magic is a process rather than a moment – lope off into a sunset, leaving behind a tawdry world of illusions and media reactions forever interdependent yet indifferent to one another's specificity.

Using images garnered from the internet and quotations from Baudrillard and Brian Eno, among others, Lundgren crafts a curious dissonant equivalence between free-market democracy and magical realism. Just as magical realism converts the describable into the improbable, Lundgren rearranges the sensible into a newly constructed image of the world that, nonetheless, articulates our suspicions about its underlying power structures. In a direct affront to formal historiography and hierarchies of knowledge, she hijacks the format of the boardroom presentation, using its authoritative aura to relate her fictions. This recalls the subterfuge of the Cold War era, where resistance was waged from within a system; and yet, ultimately confined to the gallery, it is more likely to invoke the reverie of action than the deeds themselves.

In parallel to her image and text-based work, Lundgren also conducts a performance-based practice where narrative is embellished with music and magic tricks. The series 'Meanwhile, Back At The Ranch...' (ongoing) incorporates tricks that vary in seriousness and credibility. Some are simple jokes – she transfers two matches from her mouth to her nostrils, simultaneously and hands-free, for instance – while others, like *Levitating Hat Trick*, are more enigmatic. The ascending hat carries no symbolic significance whatsoever, but contributes to the simple but confounding challenge of what is possible and what is not.

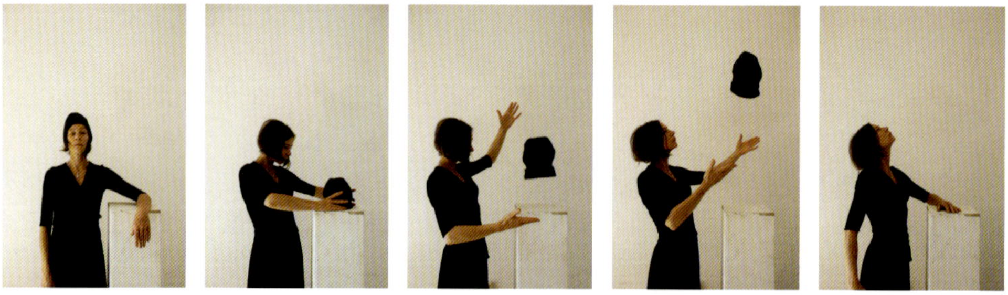

↑ *Levitating Hat Trick*, 2009

→ *Magic & Politics*, 2007

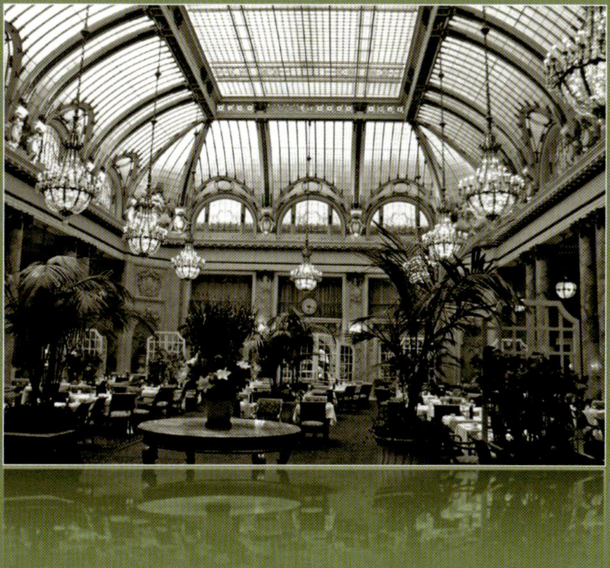

This is the convention center where the magic trick is about to take place.
The seduction lies in the details – never underestimate the power of the setup.

Juan Muñoz

JUAN Muñoz is best known for his figurative sculptural installations, where grey anonymous figures inhabit architectural space as if caught mid-narrative. But here a selection of photographic works betrays his interest in the mechanics of illusion and deception. Amongst the familiar patterned backs of playing cards we can spot tiny fingertip mirrors, known as 'shiners', which enable a card shark to surreptitiously glimpse the identity of a card. And just as the figures in Muñoz's figurative installations never quite give up the secret of their thoughts and impulses, here the framing is also left to our imagination – it is unclear whether this trickster's motivation is to con or to entertain.

Muñoz continually operated in this way, offering up fragments of actions and interactions and inviting speculation as to their nature and outcome. For him, the present becomes an arbitrary point at which to arrest the flow of time and interpret meaning. In large-scale installations such as *Double Bind* (2002) and *The Wasteland* (1987), Muñoz would orchestrate low-key snippets of intrigue and drama through the precise placement of figures within the building and in relation to one another, as well as by way of subtle gestures and stances that suggest social situations, individual states of mind and the abstract phenomena of isolation and proximity. Architectural adaptations and embellishments produce a disorientating sense of improbability or an intimate contemplative experience as viewers are led through illusory and real space, and are proffered images of human activity that are at once familiar and remote. It is as though we too are scripted, our patterns of perception made apparent through their pre-emption and headed off by blankness and irresolution.

The image of a group of men playing cards around a table that appears within *Double Bind* echoes in the sculptural realm an earlier collaboration with composer Gavin Bryars, *A Man In A Room Gambling* (1992), originally intended for radio broadcast. In a series of ten five-minute audio pieces Muñoz explains card tricks and sleights of hand over almost pastoral compositions. By appropriating the information-led format made familiar by BBC coastal weather forecasts or instructional programmes, the broadcasts signal another level at which our reading is being directed. Here the possibility for intrigue and infamy is passed on through knowledge and an atmosphere stripped of imagery.

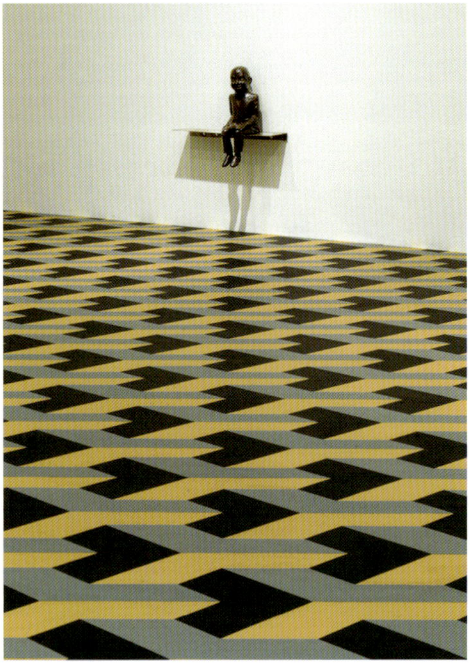

↑ *The Wasteland*, 1987
→ *Untitled*, 1995 (detail)

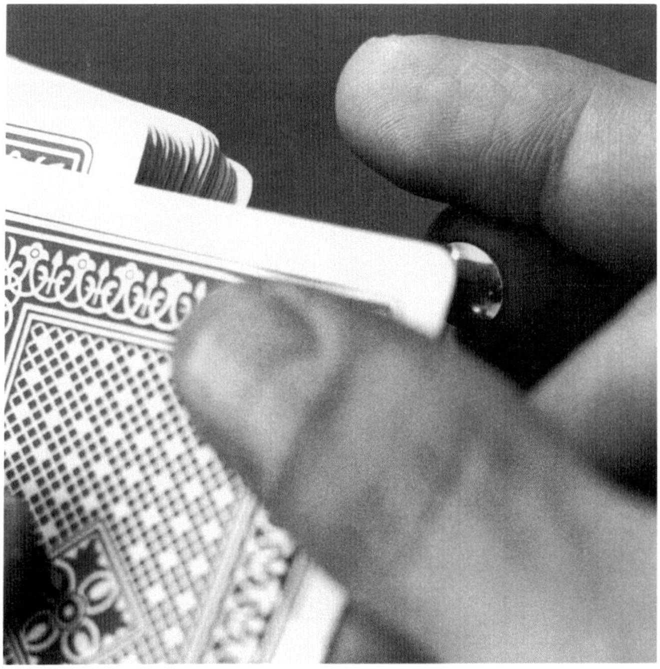

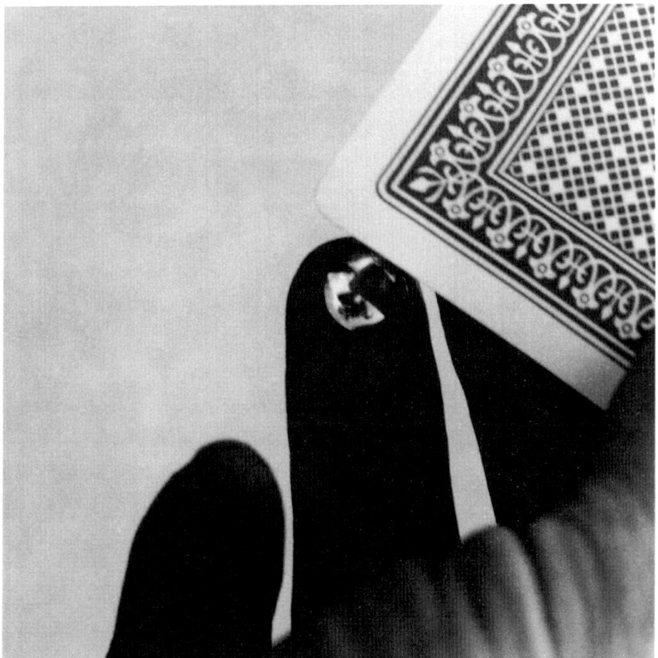

Bruce Nauman

In the late 1960s and early '70s, Bruce Nauman devised a series of mental exercises, including one in which he attempted to levitate between two chairs in his studio. The mysterious and highly charged atmosphere of the resulting double-exposed photograph is riven by skeptical pragmatism, and we are left wondering as to the nature of Nauman's belief in intangible forces and psychic agency. Indeed, throughout his long-standing and variform practice Nauman has continually withheld information pertaining to the image, phrase, form or action in hand. In the related video pieces made a few years later – *Elke Allowing the Floor to Rise Up Over Her, Face Up* (1973) and *Tony Sinking Into the Floor, Face Up and Face Down* (1973), for example – the documentation cannot reveal that Elke broke out into a sweat and Tony 'started to choke and almost got the dry heaves' during their intense experiences. As Tony explained: 'I just tried to do it too fast and I was afraid I couldn't get out'. These pieces were intended as an examination of 'a purely mental activity as opposed to a purely physical situation which might incur some mental activity',[1] and an attempt to employ the brain as a source of palpable power and influence.

The failure inherent in these lens-based documents is something that Nauman courts throughout a practice that encompasses drawing, sculpture, installation, neon, sound, film, video, text and spoken word. Deadpan slapstick thrives on failure, clumsiness and the gracelessness of human nature that periodically shows through despite all our efforts to the contrary. Unlike the magician, who performs daily hand exercises to develop the uncommon and undetectable dexterity required for sleight-of-hand tricks, Nauman amplifies the mechanics of movement in *Falls, Pratfalls and Sleights of Hand* (1993), where slipping on a banana skin or making a balloon dog become near-regal actions. As is often the case, the artist has removed these actions from their usual narrative context, so that we are left with an image or phrase mysteriously dislodged from the world of meaning – all the better to reflect on the arbitrary nature of meaning itself.

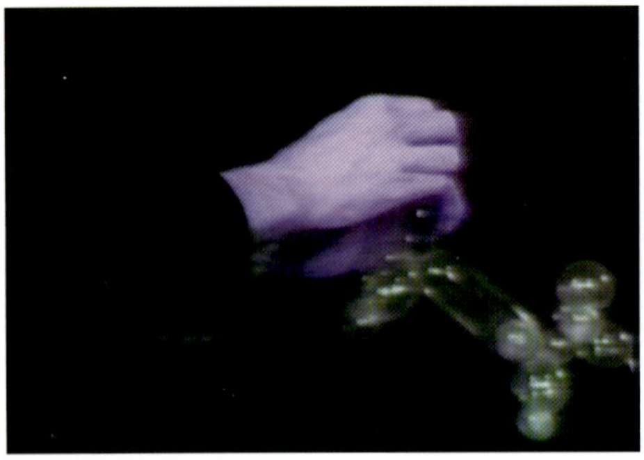

↑ *Falls, Pratfalls and Sleights of Hand (Clean Version)*, 1993 (video still)

→ *Failing to Levitate*, 1966

[1] All quotes from interview with Jan Butterfield, 1975, Janet Kraynak (ed.), *Please Pay Attention Please: Bruce Nauman's Words. Writings and interviews*, MIT Press, Cambridge, Mass., 2003, pp. 175–77.

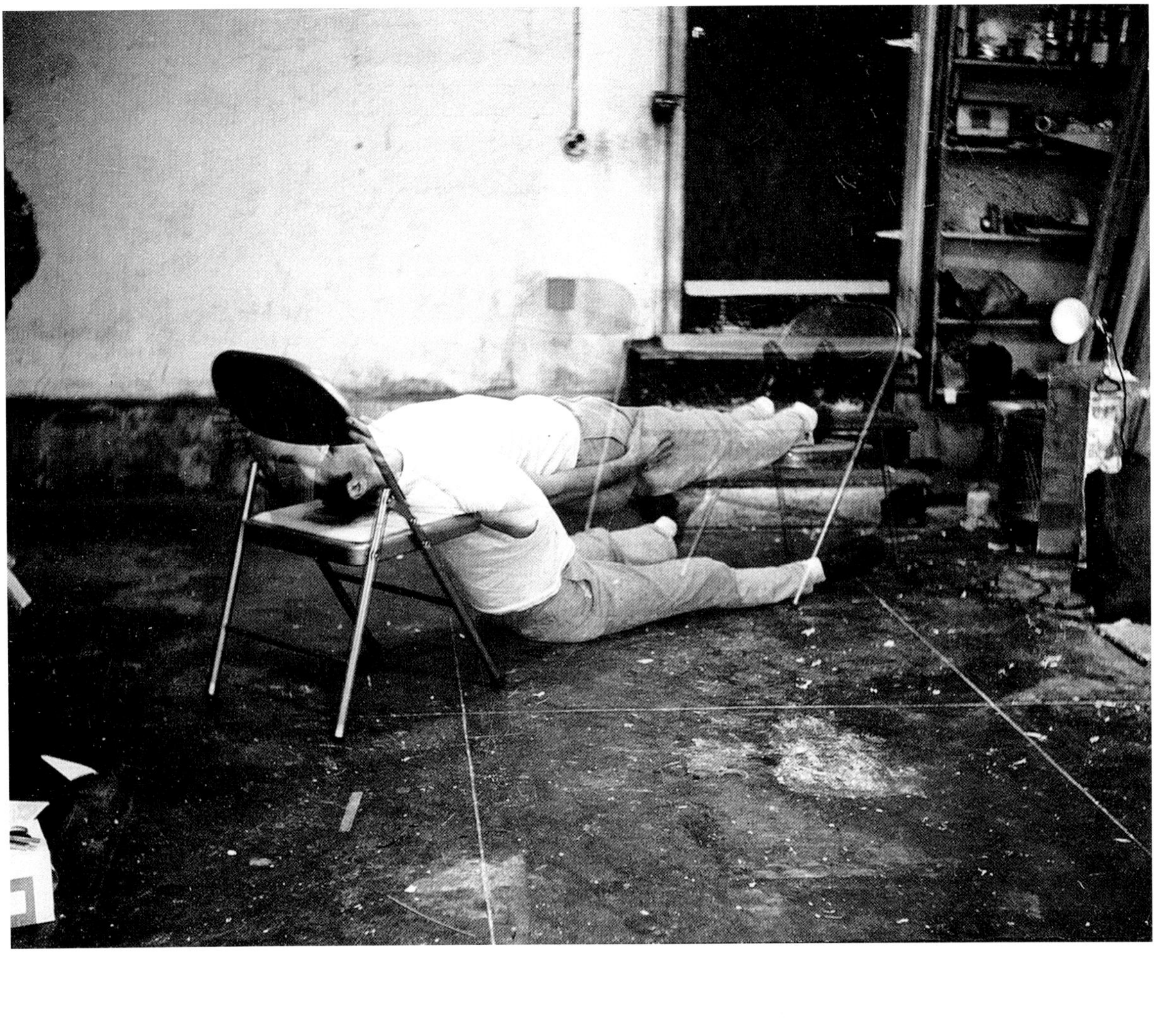

Ian Saville

Ian: So Karl, is there anything you'd like to say to the people assembled here?

Karl: Yes, I'd like to say 'all previous magicians have only interpreted the world, the point, however, is to change it.'

Ian: Well, I'm sure these people will change it. [*Looks at audience.*] Not immediately, though. Because sometimes this act is so effective that when I say to people 'change the world', they immediately want to get out there and change things. So they leave. Sometimes whole audiences react like that. Sometimes even before I've said it. Sometimes people anticipate that I'm *going* to say it, so they don't come in the first place. So you should wait until the end of the show, then go out and change things. Maybe not tonight, and tomorrow's Sunday. So, Monday. [*Turns back to Karl Marx.*] So anyway, Karl is there anything else you'd like to say?

Karl: Well, actually, I'd quite like to do a magic trick.

Ian: A magic trick?

Karl: Yes.

Ian: What sort of magic trick?

Karl: It's a sort of *prediction.*

Ian: A prediction? Is there anything you need for this?

Karl: I need to be blindfolded.

Ian: Blindfolded? Well, I've got this blindfold here, but I don't know if it will fit you.

Karl: It should do. You made it for me.

Ian: You're not supposed to tell people that.

Karl: Well, I'm trying to demystify things.

Ian: In that case, we're working at cross-purposes. [*Ian succeeds in putting the blindfold on the Karl Marx picture.*] Now, can you see anything?

Karl: Not a thing. Not a surplus value anywhere.

Ian: What do you want me to do?

Karl: I'd like you, Ian, to go out into the audience and get somebody to select a card.

Ian: Right. [*Ian leans the Karl Marx picture against a prop on his table and moves away from it.*] But there's a problem here. You see, all the lights are focused on the stage. And if I go out into the auditorium, it'll just be you up here to keep people amused and entertained. Can you do something to keep people entertained while I'm out there?

Karl: Yes. I can speak without moving my lips.

Ian: That was very good. I can only see the corner moving, and I am very close to you.

Around this wry exchange with a Karl Marx ventriloquist puppet, Ian Saville's cabaret act incorporates such socialist magic classics as the 'class-struggle rope trick' and the 'surplus value factory box' to further demonstrate ideological conundrums. Saville has performed for over 25 years on picket lines, at benefits and at many labour movement events, conferences and meetings, as well as at comedy clubs, theatres, universities and art institutions in the UK and overseas. Through the patter of the travelling showman he conveys ideology using the language of spectacle and comedy, exercising the view that the progressive left might broadcast its beliefs and aspirations more effectively through entertainment and positivity rather than through its traditional strategies of didacticism and negation.

→ *Karl Marx ventriloquist prop (second version)*, c.1980

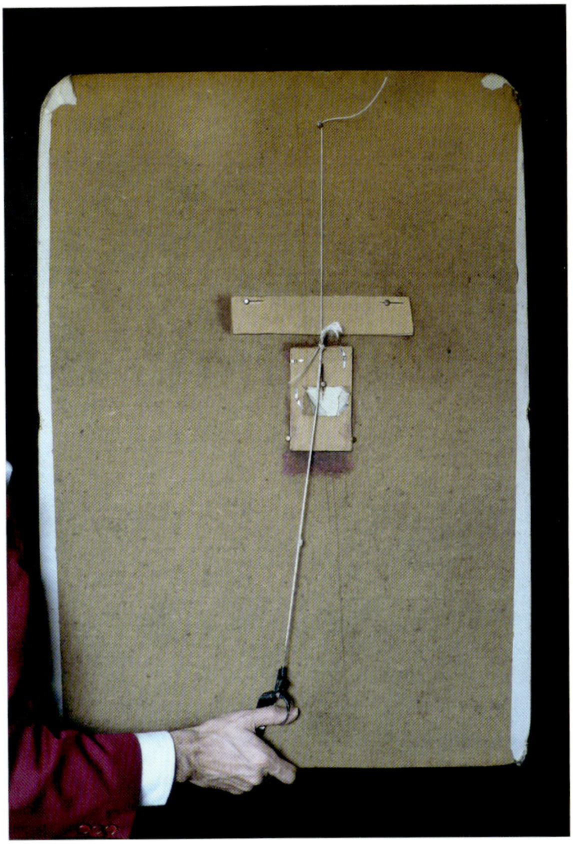

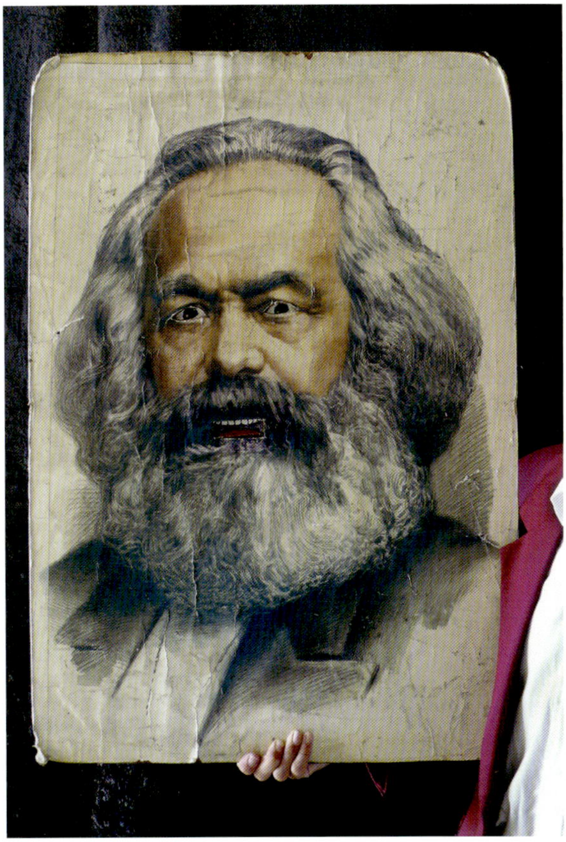

Ariel Schlesinger

Two sheets of paper lean into one another and spin steadily, as if entranced or otherwise compelled. Their dancefloor – far from an enchanted platform of desire – is a sheet of wood held aloft by four old spray cans. Ariel Schlesinger's *L'angoisse de la page blanche* [The anguish of the white page] appeals to the romanticism of the mass-produced workaday object and the genius of improvisation in the garden shed, rather than glitz or ghostliness. *L'angoisse...* makes no attempt to disguise the causal apparatus of its movement. The wires and motor that comprise the artwork's underbelly (or perhaps its exposed offal) may speak frankly of their nature, diverting mystery towards pure mechanics, but the piece is nonetheless captivating through its fragile equilibrium.

Schlesinger's prevailing aesthetic of inventive contingency reminds us of how technology has developed over centuries, through the momentum of need, the generation of desire, and the sheer happenstance of accidents. His bubble and burn machine – which produces soapy bubbles that fall into a glowing electric grill where they burst appallingly into flames – is the epitome of the pointless contraption, but is nonetheless beguiling through the economy of means by which it simulates birth and death, creation and destruction.

For the magician, too, sensational disappearances or transformations are engineered using domestic banalities: elastic bands, a safety pin, a well-placed black cloth. Schlesinger makes these contrivances not only visible but central. He talks of bringing knowable objects to a point of disaster so that they might be redeemed by the beauty of survival or transformation. Interlocking rolls of tape, tin footballers dangerously sparking on contact and a pair of gracefully curved pencils suggest events that have ended their life of usefulness, only to be resurrected by creative reconfiguration. While the blank page and sharpened pencil are votives of potential, here their prescribed application is redirected. In *L'angoisse...* the nature of this redirection is apparent, if not logically explained; in the pencils it is latent and ultimately mysterious. In both cases, though, the consumable mass-produced item becomes a prototype, reinvented through the very process of alienation, just as the magic trick demands that we consider the hidden potential of its commonplace props.

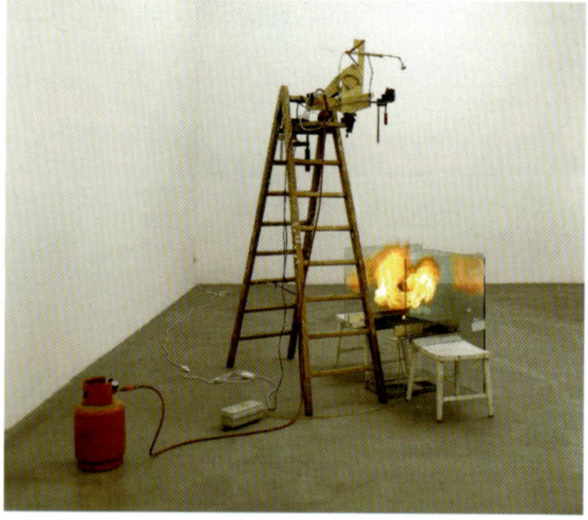

↑ *Bubble Machine*, 2006

→ *Netally and I*, 2006

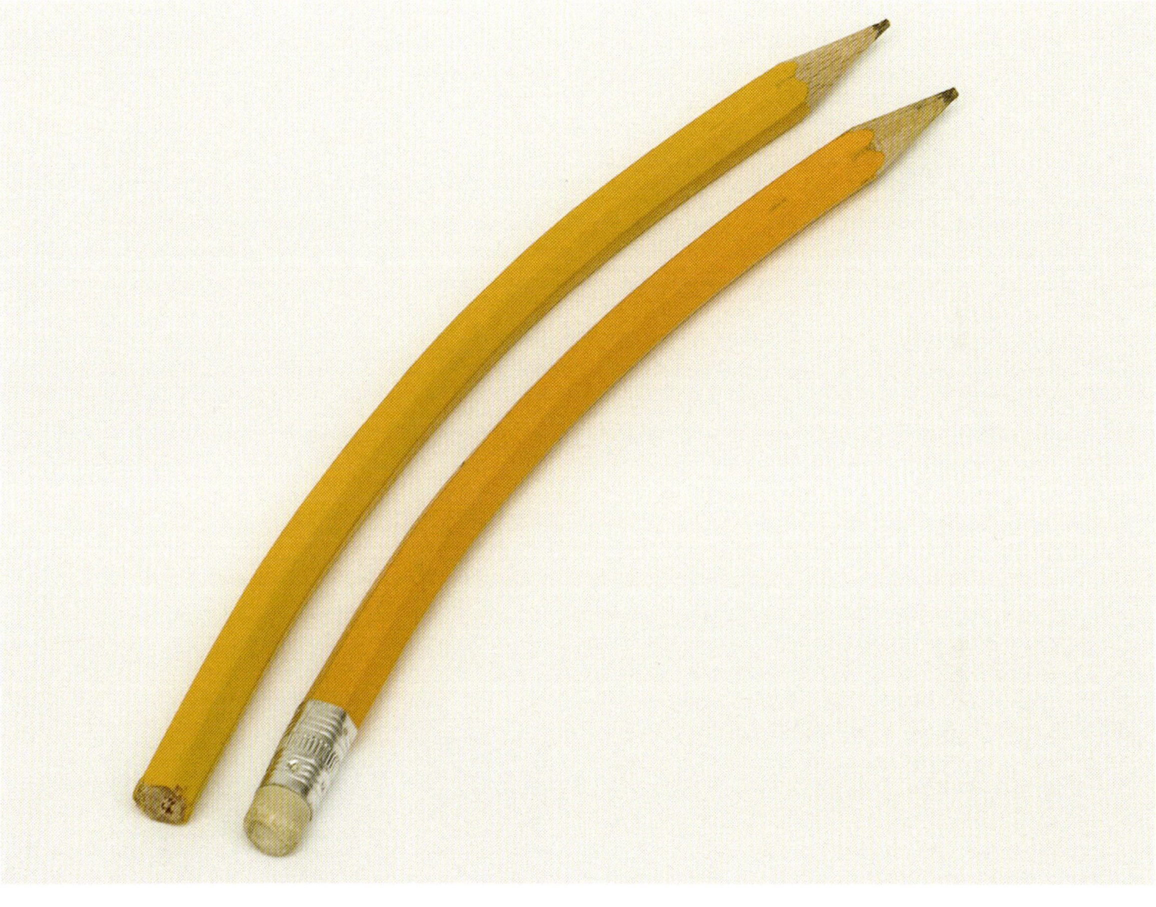

Suzanne Treister

SUZANNE Treister evokes the unstable, even hallucinatory, nature of history and identity. Investigating and provoking through means that recall those of the alchemist and the occultist, she represents real-world structures that are more usually inscribed by orthodox, contemporary modes of power. Mass media, party politics and the military are viewed through the filter of esoteric philosophy of the 16th and 17th centuries, when interconnectivity was of a different order to the secular, manmade information highways of today.

Treister's large watercolours that make up the series *Alchemy* (2007-8) are a giddying graphic translation of mainstream international print media, where the headlines, body text and photojournalism of newspaper front pages are rendered in the schematic iconography of a bygone era. This process of transmutation, while making no claims to reveal underlying truth or teleological forces, casts a light on news that is at once alienating and revelatory. Authorship, reportage and the creation of meaning are, Treister implies, as spuriously configured as defunct knowledge structures. The place of rumour, conspiracy theories and the manipulation of words and action become as legitimate as those former heresies that have, since the Enlightenment, been reappraised as the glimmers of scientific fact.

Whereas alchemists searched for signifiers of hidden meaning, Treister analogously wields their processes as a form of institutional critique. While many of her projects approach very real situations where issues of covert influence and manipulation do indeed need to be addressed – as in *HEXEN2039* (2006), when Treister's alter ego, the delusional time traveller Rosalind Brodsky, elaborates on military-occult technologies for psychological warfare – others are entirely flights of fancy. The *Gematria* series (2009) , for instance, is a self-consciously paranoid exercise where names of Jewish magicians, the FBI's most wanted and attendees of a series of conferences on cybernetics are translated in Hebrew and the numerical equivalent of their composite letters calculated. As Treister explains, this is to gain insight into and explore interrelationships between concepts, language and meaning; although, again, this is not to extrapolate belief in cabbalistic or magical formulas into inappropriate arenas. Rather, it prompts rumination on such procedures and their subject matter, as they toy with transformative power and the production of knowledge.

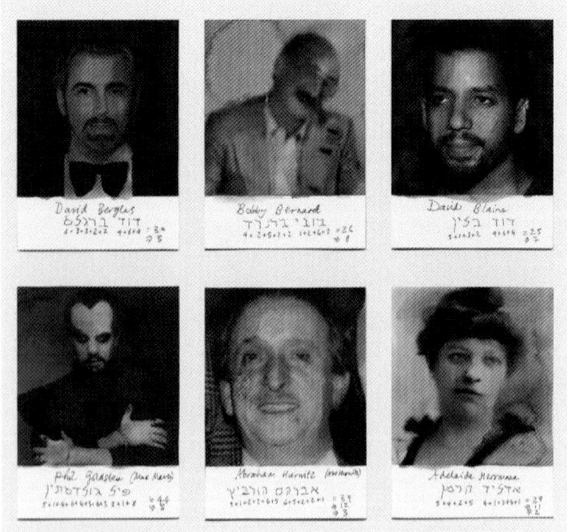

↑ *GEMATRIA/40 Jewish Magicians*, 2009 (detail)

→ *ALCHEMY/Al-Ahram, 31st January – 6th February 2008*, 2008

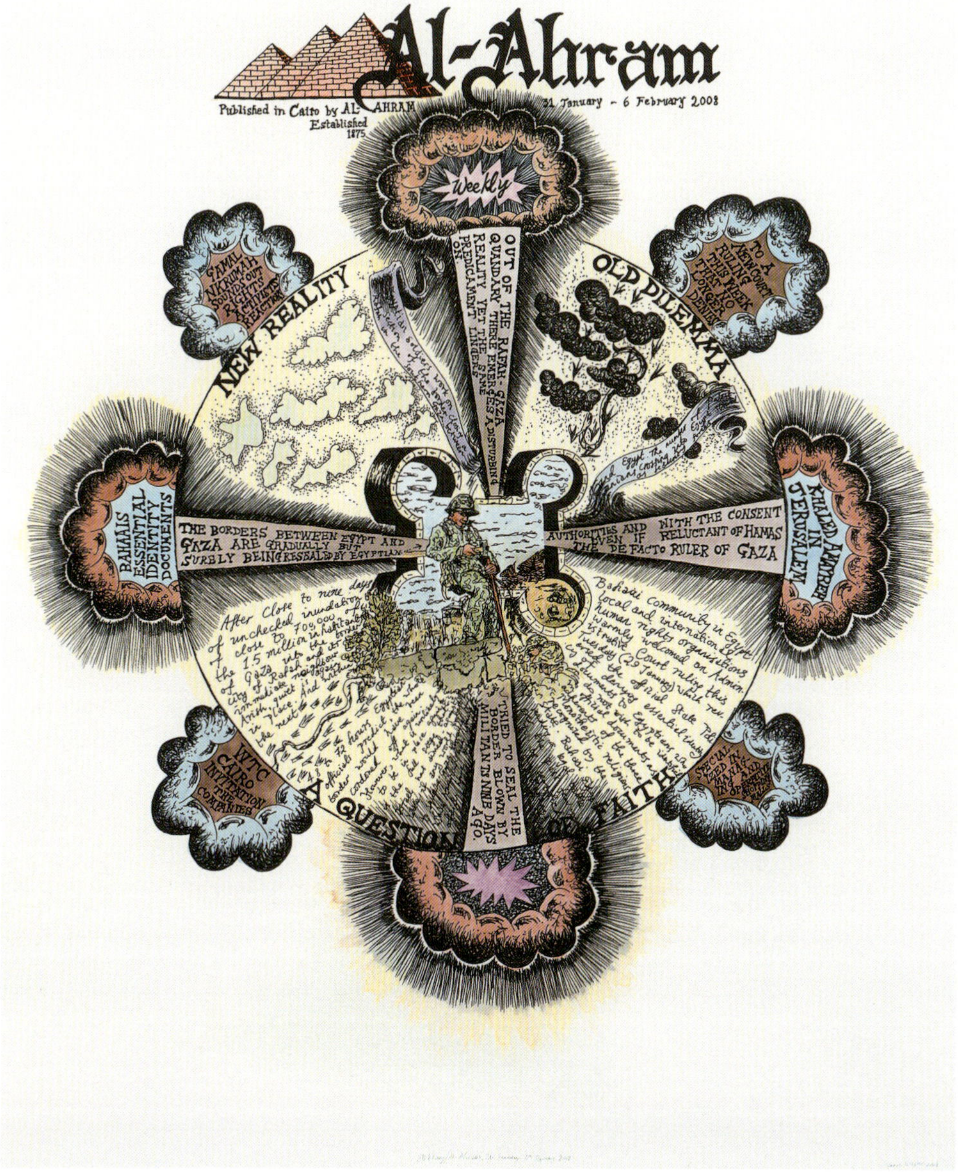
Al-Ahram
Published in Cairo by AL-AHRAM
Established 1875
31 January - 6 February 2008
Weekly
OUT OF THE RAFAH-GAZA QUANDARY THERE EMERGES A DISTURBING REALITY YET THE PREDICAMENT LINGERS ON
NEW REALITY
OLD DILEMMA
THE BORDERS BETWEEN EGYPT AND GAZA ARE GRADUALLY BUT SURELY BEING RESEALED BY EGYPTIAN
AUTHORITIES AND WITH THE CONSENT EVEN IF RELUCTANT OF HAMAS THE DE FACTO RULER OF GAZA
BAHAIS ESSENTIAL IDENTITY DOCUMENTS
KHALED AMAYREH IN JERUSALEM
TRIED TO SEAL THE BORDER BLOWN BY MILITANTS NINE DAYS AGO.
A QUESTION OF FAITH
WTC CAIRO
COMPANIES

Sinta Werner

SINTA Werner's installations are not so much site-specific as site-reflexive. If there is an element that is 'specific', though, it is the position at which the viewer stands to make sense of what otherwise appears to be the architectural embodiment of seasickness. Like the anamorphic skull in Holbein's *The Ambassadors* (1533), Werner's structural interruptions snap into a logically comprehensible form only when she has us where she wants us. The rest of the time the three-dimensional representation of space is more likely to generate feelings of disorientation, irritation, even vertigo, not least of all because from the mathematical and precise she creates something illogical and mysterious.

Werner's architectonic installations dissolve together the genres of image, sculpture and architecture. Developed from the single-point perspective of traditional illusory painting and Alberti's model of the visual pyramid, their subversion of the *a priori* of picture making recalls the painterly concerns of cubism and the instability of post-modernism in the latter half of the 20th century, when authority and belief gave way to an acknowledgement of the contingent construction of meaning. And yet many of these effects are achieved through methods not dissimilar to those of long-established stage crafts such as foreshortening and mimetic *trompe l'oeil*.

Mirroring, too, is a fundamental process that Werner wields to create complex physiological and psychological effects. *Disjunction* (2007), for instance, produces the sensation of approaching a mirror in which the self does not appear. Through this uncanny disappearance we are likely to reflect on the performative nature of our behaviour within the real exhibition space, as it compels us to step to the side or peer round a corner to check what is 'really going on'. But for Werner it also refers to Foucault's idea of heterotopias – where the mirror is a metaphor for the reality and illusion of utopias – as well as to places such as gardens or museums, where objects from many times and places converge artificially. Notionally, it could be argued that Werner brings no alien object into the gallery, but merely re-presents what is already there. But that this illusion of absence produces such disturbing results foregrounds the sophisticated processes of assimilation we continually perform to overcome the fragmentation and decentredness of everyday life.

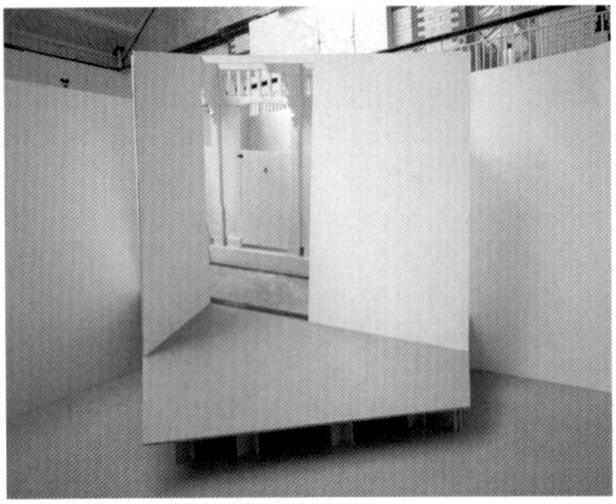

↑ *Disjunction*, 2007

→ Model for a site-specific installation at QUAD, Derby and The Grundy Gallery, Blackpool, 2009

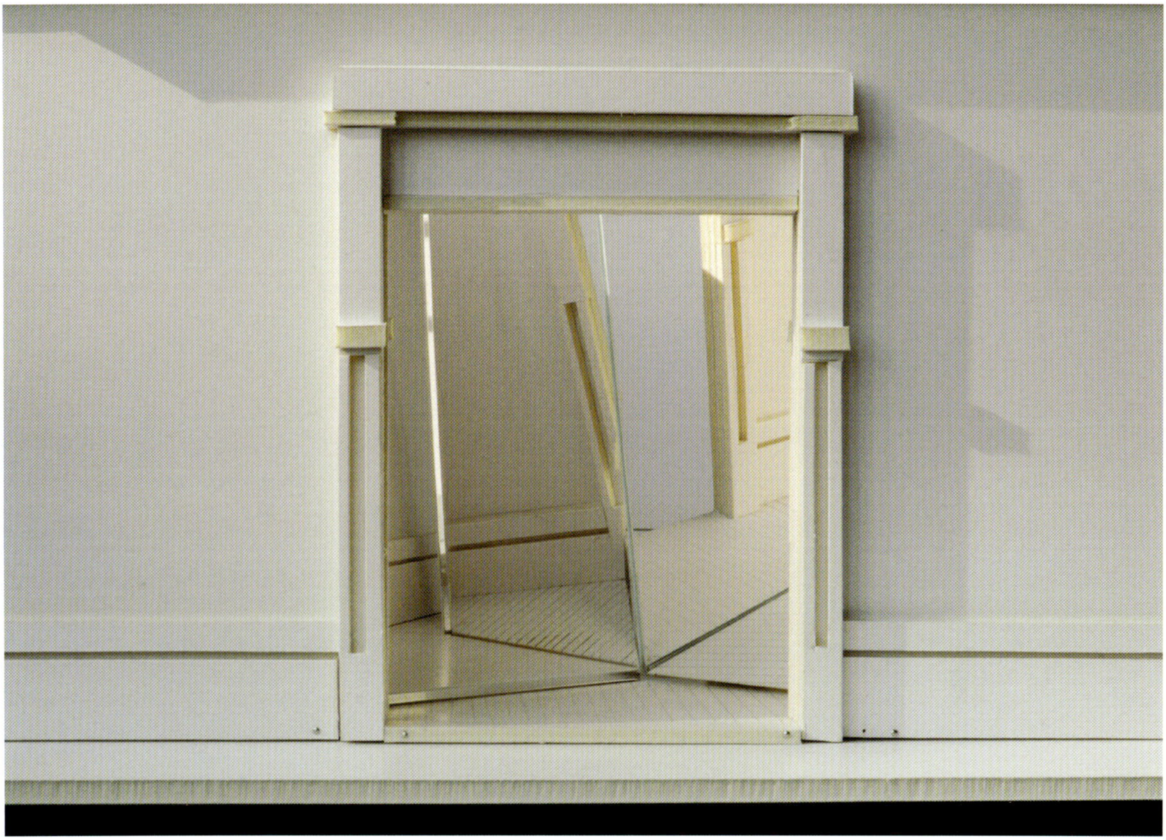

Conjuring Consent

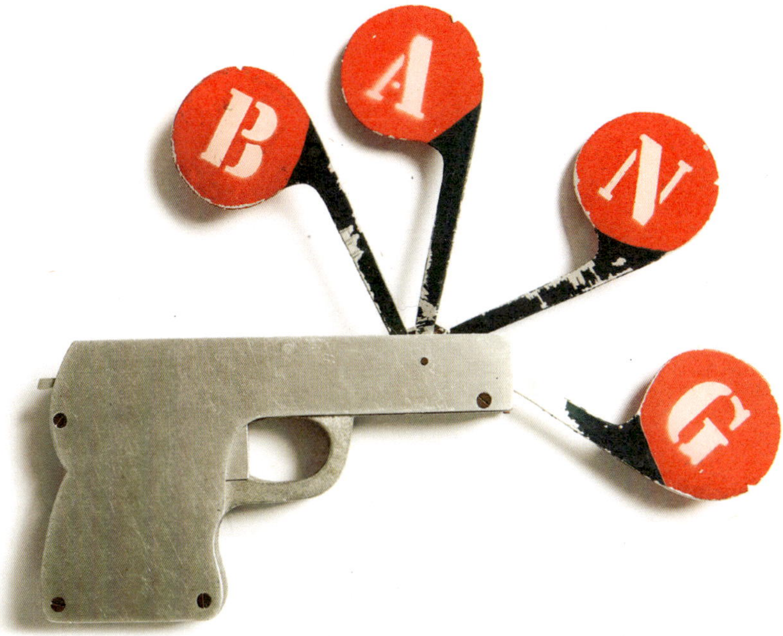

Conventionally the theatrical magician's remit is to entertain. The selection of artefacts presented here, on the other hand, demonstrates how magic can also be used to more emotive or divisive ends when deployed in specific contexts.

By manipulating our understanding of the world, the magician might activate political or ethical programmes, conjure our unquestioning consent or persuade us to consume or condone that which we ordinarily might not.

Conventional Props

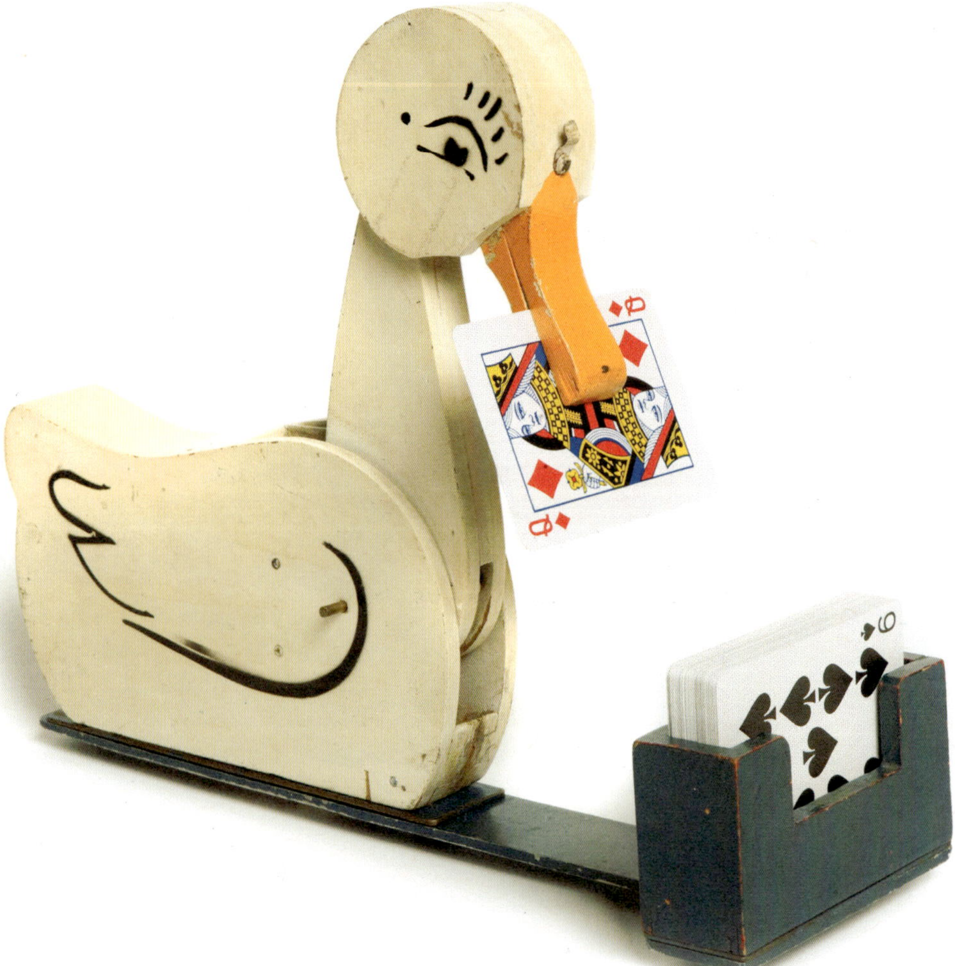

Previous page: **Bang Gun, 1950s**

Fictitious firearms often appear on the magic stage, most commonly in the form of the impotent 'bang gun'. The lack of brand markings and unusual design in this example suggest that the item was custom-made by or for its user.

1. 'Card-Finding Duck', c.1970

The duck's beak is designed to recover a freely chosen playing card from a shuffled deck. This example was formerly owned by British magician Tommy Cooper (1924–1984).

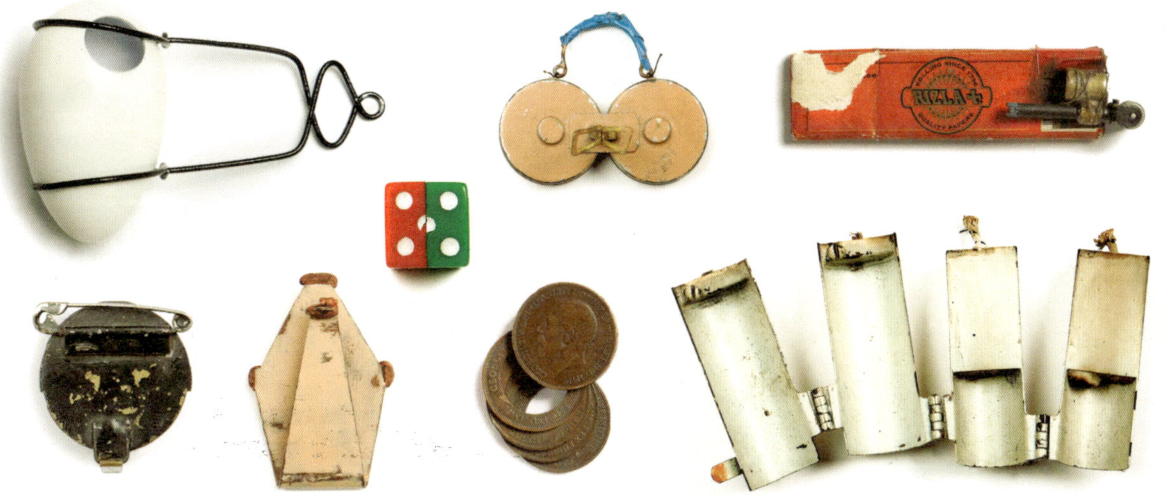

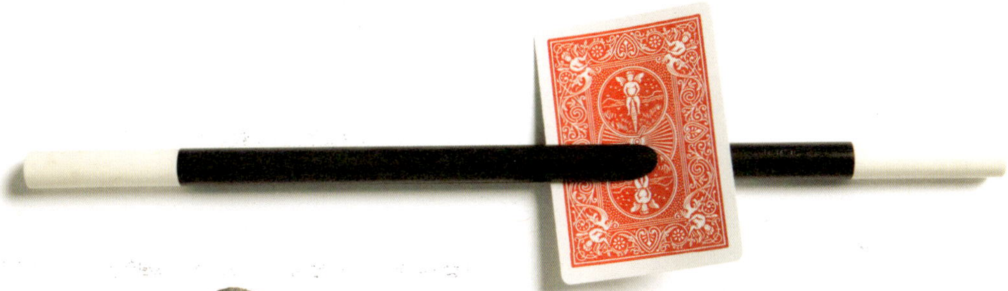

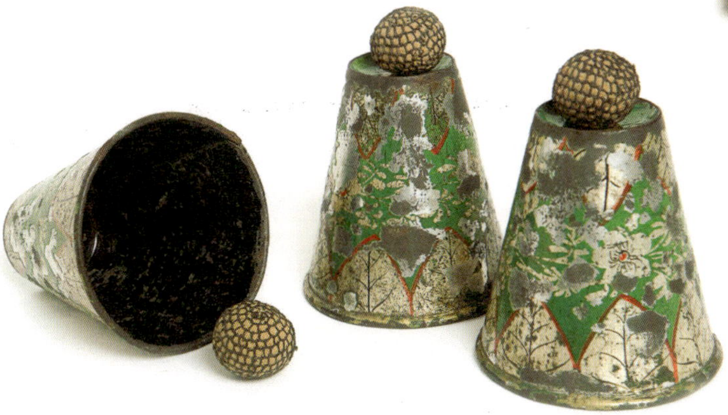

2. A selection of magician's 'gimmicks', 1970s–90s

Described by magician Jean Bobo as 'shortcuts to the supernatural', such devices are the hidden technical components behind many magic effects.

3. 'Wand through Card', c.1960

A traditional magician's wand designed to pass freely through a selected playing card without tearing it.

4. Cups and Balls, late 19th century

The 'Cups and Balls' is one of magic's most enduring tricks, and has come to represent a rite of passage for aspiring performers. The cork balls used in this Japanese set are webbed to provide extra grip.

Political Magic

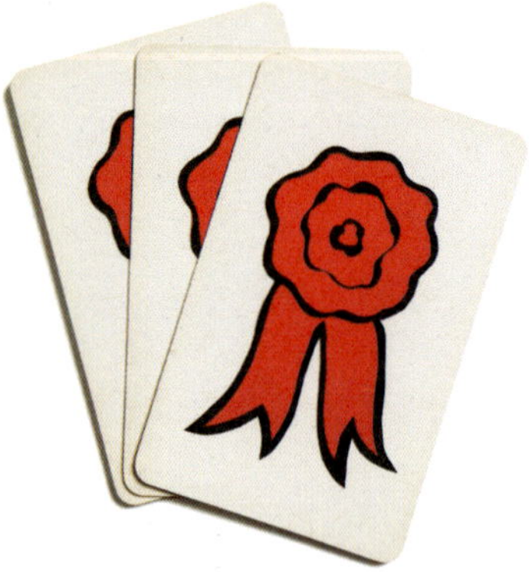

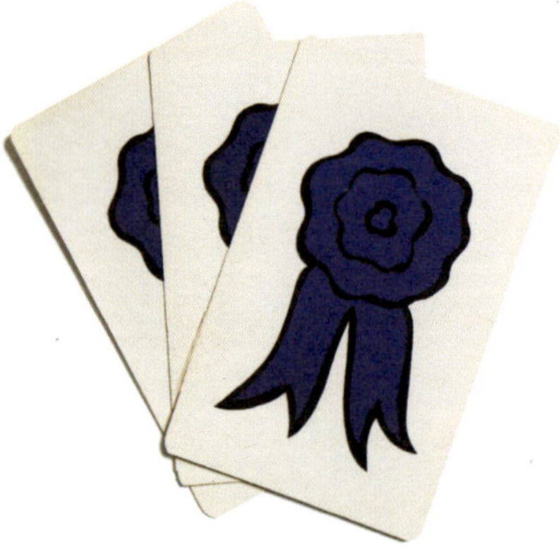

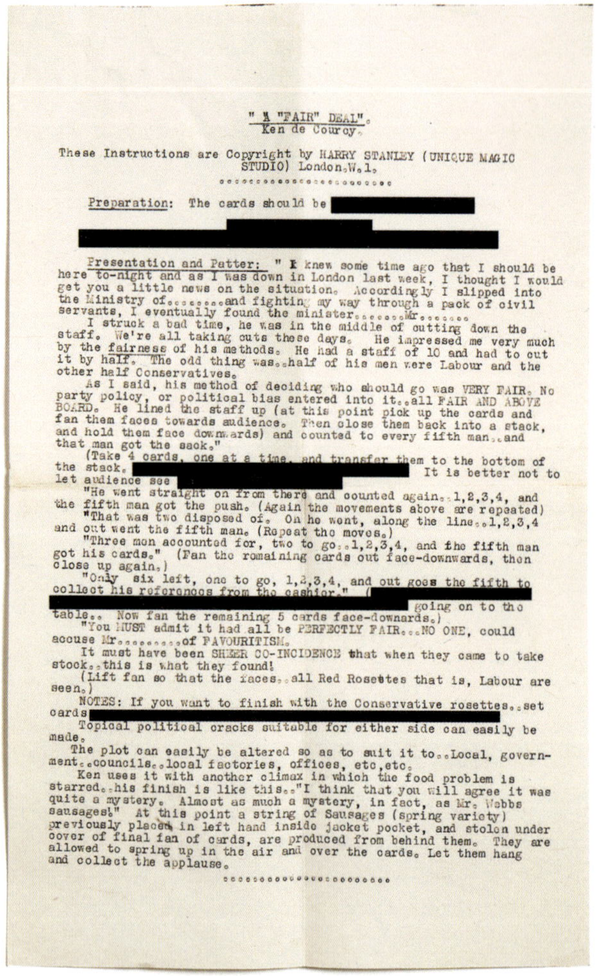

" A "FAIR" DEAL".
Ken de Courcy.

These Instructions are Copyright by HARRY STANLEY (UNIQUE MAGIC STUDIO) London.W.1.

oooooooooooooooooooooooo

Preparation: The cards should be [redacted]

Presentation and Patter: " I knew some time ago that I should be here to-night and as I was down in London last week, I thought I would get you a little news on the situation. Accordingly I slipped into the Ministry of.........and fighting my way through a pack of civil servants, I eventually found the minister........Mr........

I struck a bad time, he was in the middle of cutting down the staff. We're all taking cuts these days. He impressed me very much by the fairness of his methods. He had a staff of 10 and had to cut it by half. The odd thing was..half of his men were Labour and the other half Conservatives.

As I said, his method of deciding who should go was VERY FAIR. No party policy, or political bias entered into it..all FAIR AND ABOVE BOARD. He lined the staff up (at this point pick up the cards and fan them faces towards audience. Then close them back into a stack, and hold them face downwards) and counted to every fifth man..and that man got the sack."

(Take 4 cards, one at a time, and transfer them to the bottom of the stack. [redacted] It is better not to let audience see [redacted]

"He went straight on from there and counted again..1,2,3,4, and the fifth man got the push. (Again the movements above are repeated)

"That was two disposed of. On he went, along the line..1,2,3,4 and out went the fifth man. (Repeat the moves.)

"Three men accounted for, two to go..1,2,3,4, and the fifth man got his cards." (Fan the remaining cards out face-downwards, then close up again.)

"Only six left, one to go, 1,2,3,4, and out goes the fifth to collect his references from the cashier." ([redacted] going on to the table.. Now fan the remaining 5 cards face-downwards.)

"You MUST admit it had all be PERFECTLY FAIR...NO ONE, could accuse Mr..........of FAVOURITISM.

It must have been SHEER CO-INCIDENCE that when they came to take stock..this is what they found!

(Lift fan so that the faces..all Red Rosettes that is, Labour are seen.)

NOTES: If you want to finish with the Conservative rosettes..set cards [redacted]

Topical political cracks suitable for either side can easily be made.

The plot can easily be altered so as to suit it to..Local, government..councils..local factories, offices, etc,etc.

Ken uses it with another climax in which the food problem is starred..his finish is like this.."I think that you will agree it was quite a mystery. Almost as much a mystery, in fact, as Mr. Webbs sausages!" At this point a string of Sausages (spring variety) previously placed in left hand inside jacket pocket, and stolen under cover of final fan of cards, are produced from behind them. They are allowed to spring up in the air and over the cards. Let them hang and collect the applause.

oooooooooooooooooooooooo

Politicians are famously battling for public trust and therefore rarely use the rhetoric of magic, which implies illusion, obfuscation and even deception. The stage magician nevertheless provides grist for the mill of satirists who emphasise how false claims for transparency and demonstrations of disproportionate power are widespread within both magic and politics.

1. 'A "Fair" Deal', UK, 1970s

The standard patter for this trick involves a plot in which proposed civil service job cuts are distributed 'fairly' amongst political parties, with red and blue rosettes denoting the partisan divide. The instructions suggest, however, that the plot can be easily altered to suit the requirements of local government, councils, factories, offices and so on.

Crucial passages have been censored by the editors to conceal the trick's method from unauthorised readers.

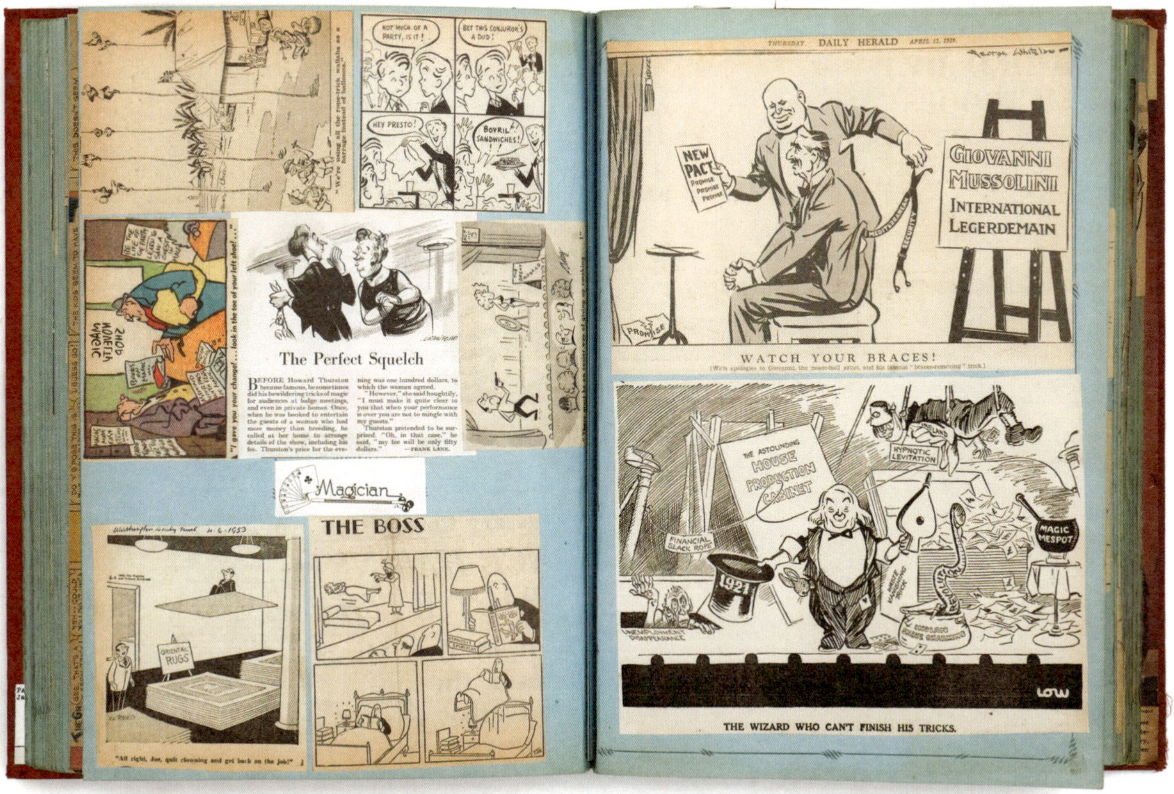

2. A scrapbook of magic-themed cartoons assembled by Stanley Collins (1881–1966) covering the period 1886 to the mid 1950s.

One of the best-known names in British magic of his time, Collins was a professional conjurer who performed at Masonic functions, banquets in the City of London and other elite engagements. He was a bibliophile and a prolific and creative contributor to the literature of his discipline, as well as an ardent collector of everything pertaining to the art of magic.

Magic and Conflict

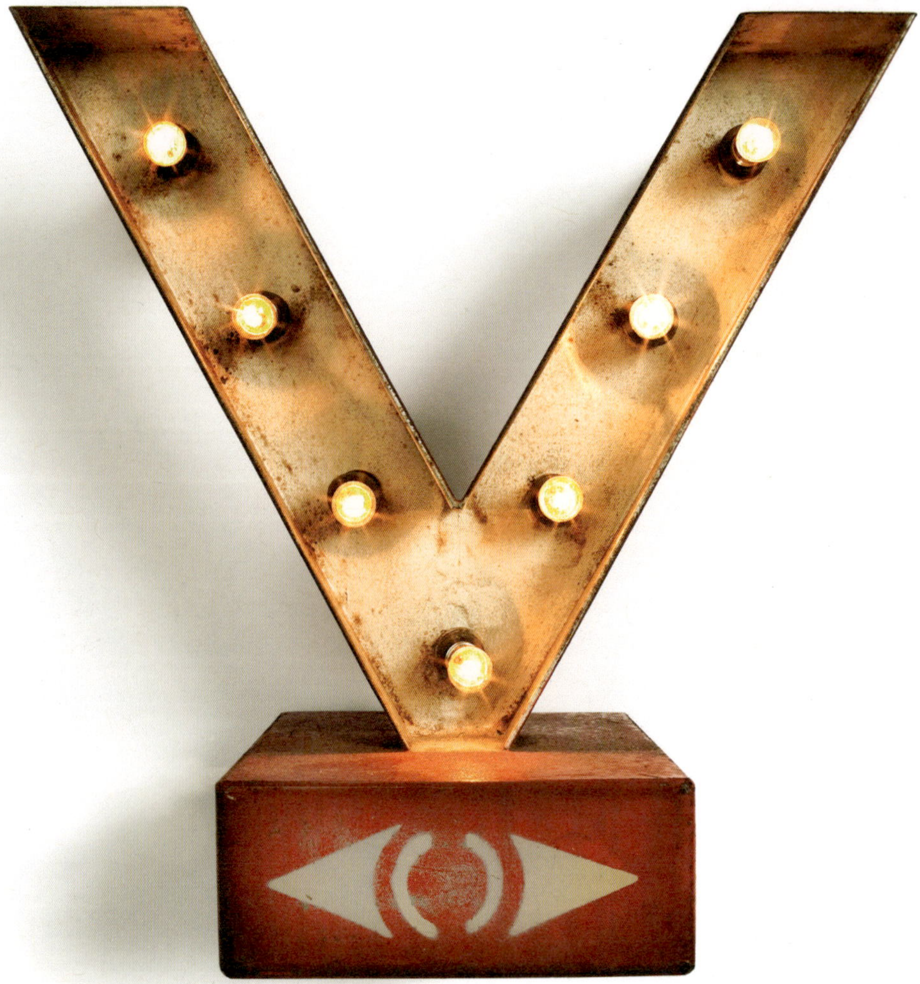

In the theatre of war magic proves a valuable resource on many fronts from entertaining the troops to illustrating propagandist ideas. Although by nature conflict encourages strategies on the ground, whereby cunning and conning become indistinct, here we concentrate on illusions employed beyond the battlefield to raise morale or instil antipathy towards the enemy.

1. 'The "Electro" Victory Stand', 1940s

This battery-operated metal prop is unusually lavish, given the scarcity of materials during the period. The magician would remove and 'swallow' each light bulb and moments later pull a string of lighted bulbs from his mouth and place it within the framework of the 'Victory V'.

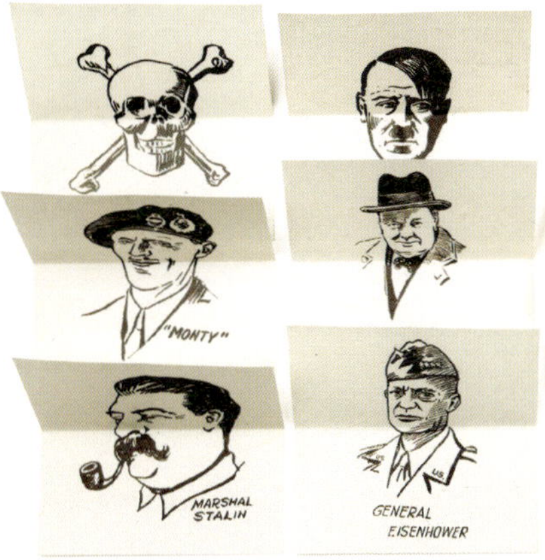

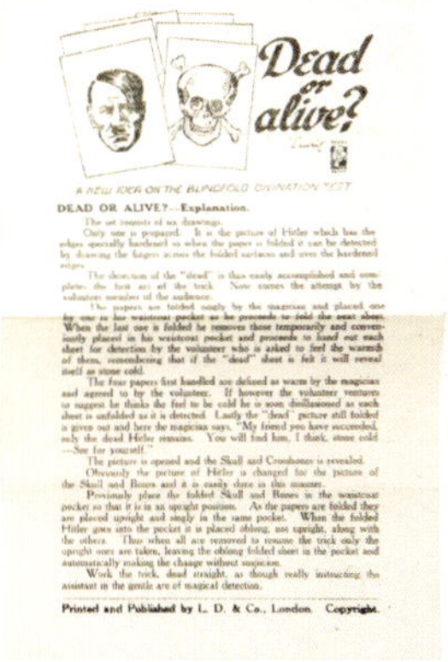
Dead or alive?

A NEW IDEA ON THE BLINDFOLD DIVINATION TEST

DEAD OR ALIVE?—Explanation.

The set consists of six drawings.

Only one is prepared. It is the picture of Hitler which has the edges specially hardened so when the paper is folded it can be detected by drawing the fingers across the folded surfaces and over the hardened edges.

The detection of the "dead" is thus easily accomplished and completes the first act of the trick. Now comes the attempt by the volunteer member of the audience.

The papers are folded singly by the magician and placed one by one in his waistcoat pocket as he proceeds to fold the next sheet. When the last one is folded he removes those temporarily and conveniently placed in his waistcoat pocket and proceeds to hand out each sheet for detection by the volunteer who is asked to feel the warmth of them, remembering that if the "dead" sheet is felt it will reveal itself as stone cold.

The four papers first handled are defined as warm by the magician and agreed to by the volunteer. If however the volunteer ventures to suggest he thinks the feel to be cold he is soon disillusioned as each sheet is unfolded as it is detected. Lastly the "dead" picture still folded is given out and here the magician says, "My friend you have succeeded, only the dead Hitler remains. You will find him, I think, stone cold —See for yourself."

The picture is opened and the Skull and Crossbones is revealed.

Obviously the picture of Hitler is changed for the picture of the Skull and Bones and it is easily done in this manner.

Previously place the folded Skull and Bones in the waistcoat pocket so that it is in an upright position. As the papers are folded they are placed upright and singly in the same pocket. When the folded Hitler goes into the pocket it is placed oblong, not upright, along with the others. Thus when all are removed to resume the trick only the upright ones are taken, leaving the oblong folded sheet in the pocket and automatically making the change without suspicion.

Work the trick, dead straight, as though really instructing the assistant in the gentle art of magical detection.

Printed and Published by L. D. & Co., London. Copyright.

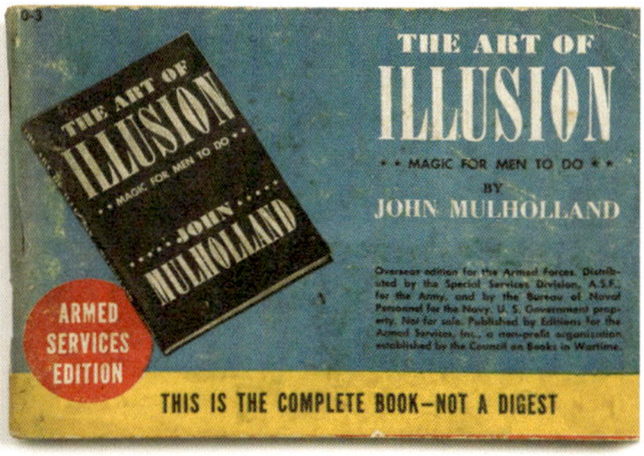

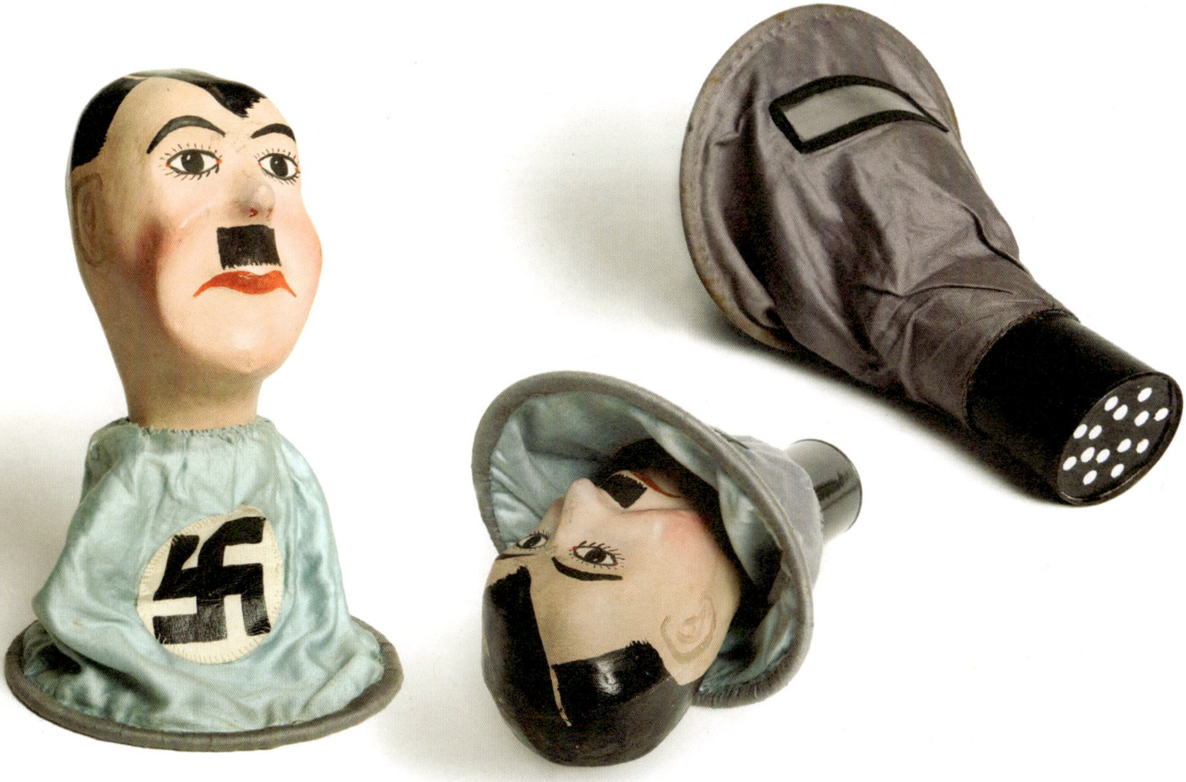

2. 'Dead or Alive', 1940s

This close-up trick, produced by Davenports Magic Company in London, involves a blindfolded magician apparently determining whether Churchill, Eisenhower, Montgomery, Stalin and Hitler are alive by the supposed warmth of the illustrated cards.

3. *The Art of Illusion* (Armed Services Edition), The Council on Books in Wartime, USA, 1944

American magician John Mulholland's popular how-to-do-magic book was republished in miniature so that it could be carried in the shirt pockets of American soldiers for their entertainment and diversion. Mulholland later assisted the CIA during the Cold War by instructing agents in close-up magic for use in the field.

4. 'Gas-mask to Gas-bag', 1940s

This reversible prop was advertised in the Davenports catalogue as a comical show opener and bore the strapline 'It's Sure – It's Swift – It's a Blitzkrieg'.

Gospel Magic

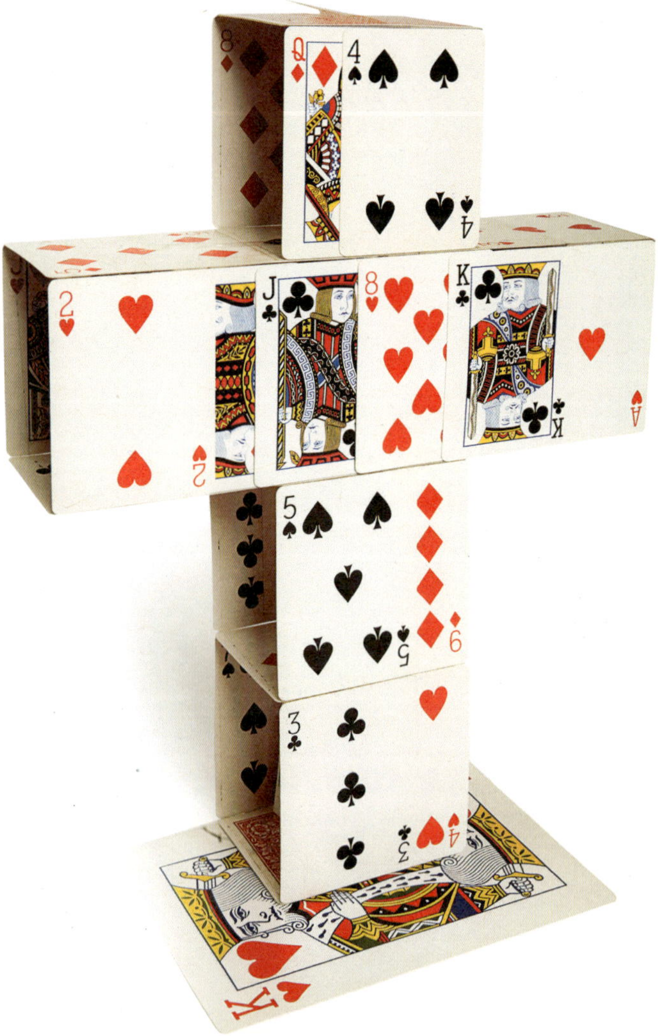

The magical and the miraculous compete in the hands of the evangelical 'gospel magician' who corrals stage-crafted illusion within his or her emotive and iconographic agenda.

1. Card cross, 1992

The wit within the theatrical armoury of the gospel magician becomes apparent in this prop, where a stack of playing cards, the 'devil's picture book', instantly configures itself as a cross-shaped card-castle. This particular card cross has accompanied its owner and inventor Dan Wolfe on performance tours worldwide since 1992.

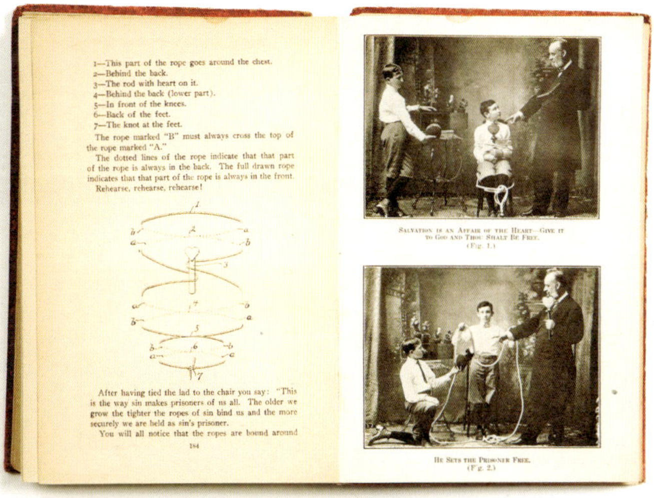

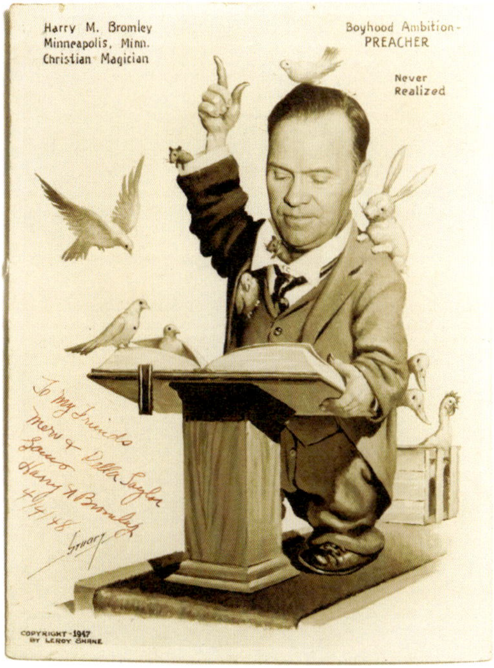

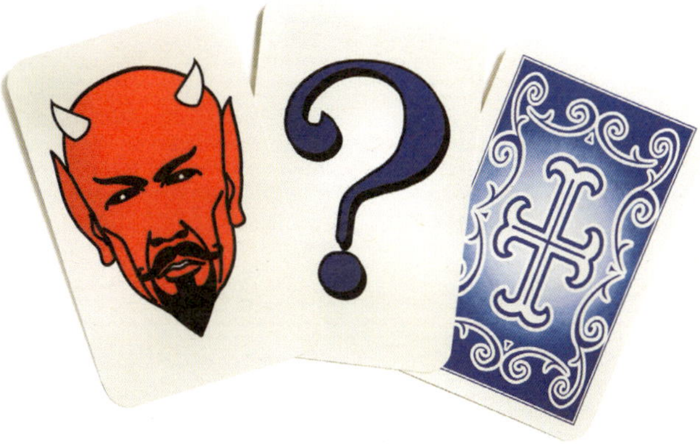

2. Rev. C.H. Woolston, *Seeing Truth: Object Lessons with Magical and Mechanical Devices*, The Praise Publishing Company, Philadelphia and Chicago, 1910.

Although the Pennsylvanian pastor C.H. Woolston is considered the father of modern gospel magic, Christian-themed magic has historical precedent in European Medieval mystery plays. Effects such as the beheading of John the Baptist or the miraculous ascension of Jesus were threatricalised using illusion techniques that are, in some cases, still used today. Here, a rope trick is reframed by Woolston as an 'object lesson' on the theme of salvation.

3. 'Harry M.Bromley/Christian Magician/Boyhood Ambition – Preacher/Never Realized', 1947

Harry Bromley's boyhood ambition to be a preacher, although 'never realised', is achieved here in a photo-montaged publicity image, where a menagerie of animals that feature often on the magic stage surround a St Francis-like Bromley preaching at a lectern.

4. 'Find Ugly', 1997

The conventional three-card monte, in which a spectator tries in vain to follow the location of one of three playing cards, here takes a diabolic turn. During performance, 'Ugly' (the devil card) is eventually found stuck to the back of the gospel magician's jacket.

Magic and Marketing

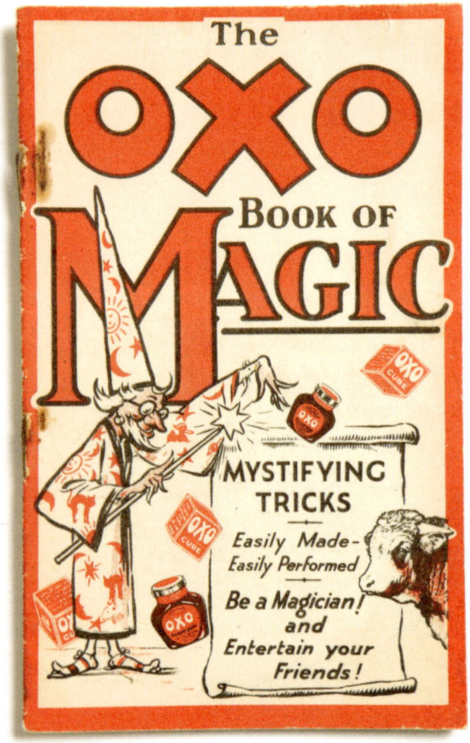

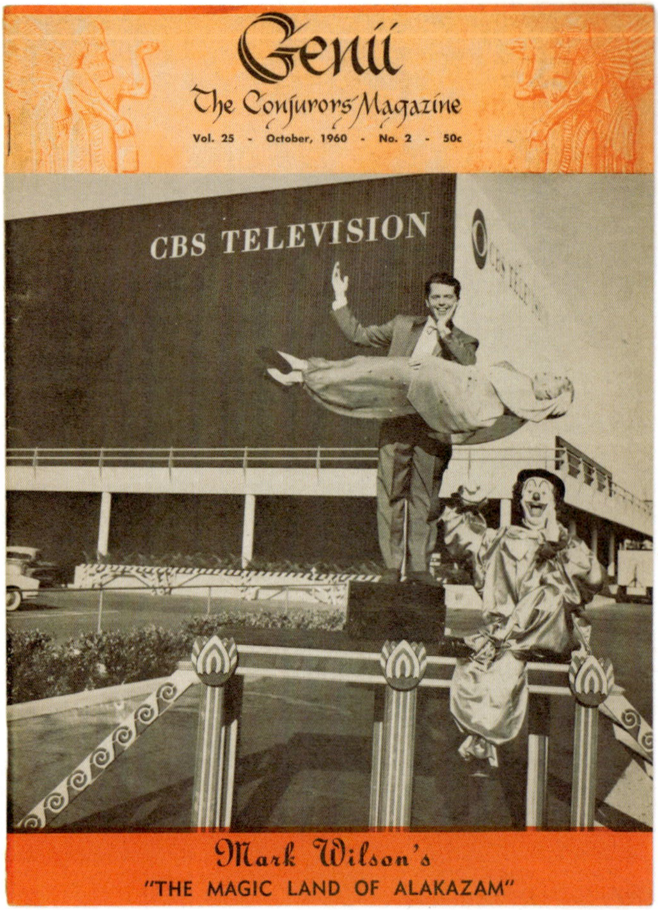

The deployment of magic in advertisements is commonly used to beguile children or engage adults by way of irony or nostalgia. Often a product claiming magical powers is simply exaggerating what is a more tasty, shiny or fragrant version than its competitors. In this way, magic in marketing is only ever allegorical, if not entirely spurious.

1. *The Oxo Book of Magic*, Oxo Ltd, London, 1934

The cover features a wizard vanishing Oxo gravy cubes while a nearby cow confronts potential young magicians with a fixed gaze. The 19-page booklet contains many magic effects that make use of Oxo-cube boxes and other related products.

2. *Genii – The Conjuror's Magazine*, 1960

Magician Mark Wilson and his wife Nani Darnell, shown here on the cover of *Genii* magazine, were key figures in the establishment of the magic show as a television format. *The Magic Land of Allakazam* (1960-2) was broadcast on CBS and sponsored by Kellogg's.

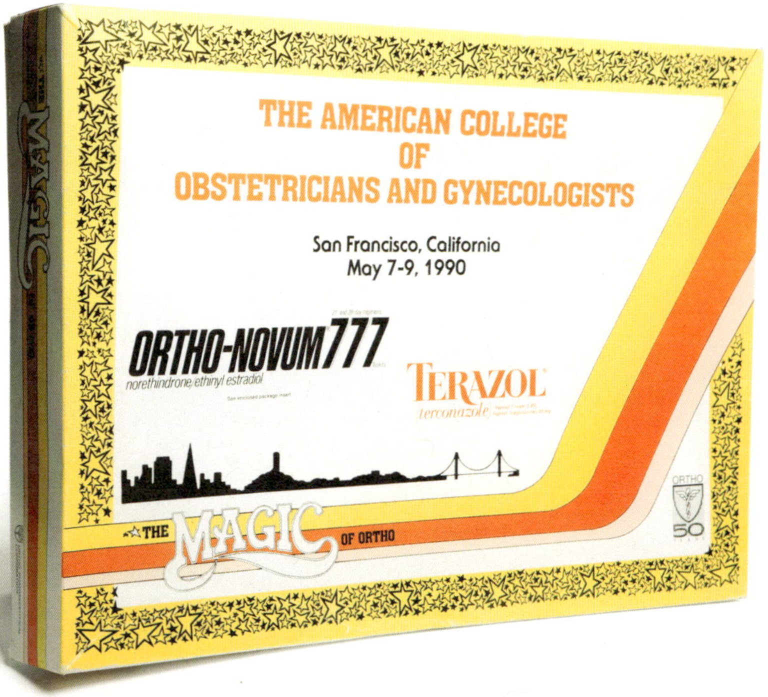

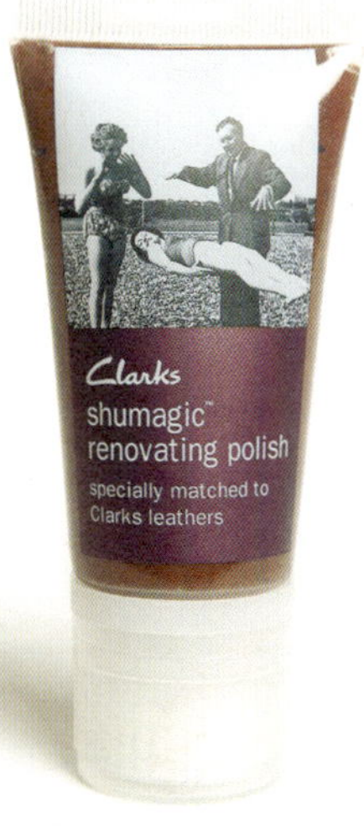

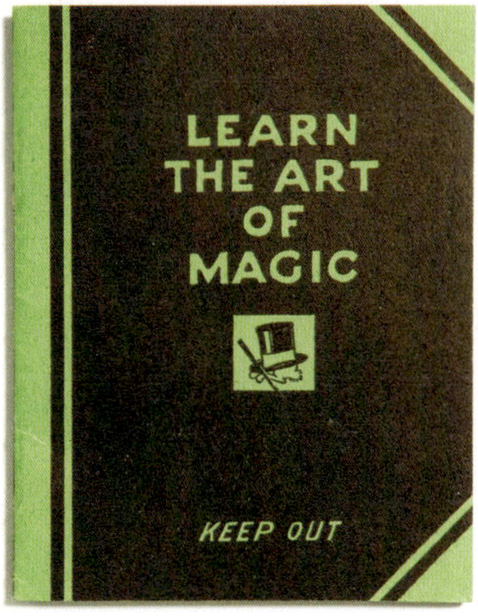

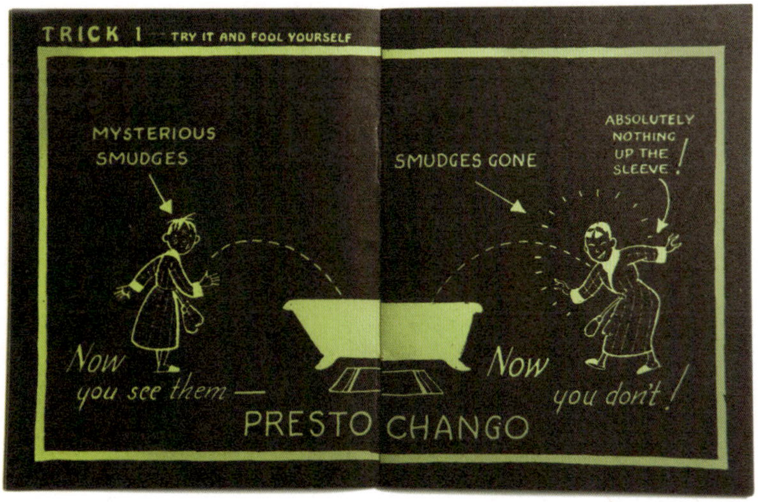

During the show, Wilson would often appear magically from within a human-size box of breakfast cereal and request the studio audience join him in the magic word 'Kellogg's!'

3. *The Magic of Ortho*, 1990

This magic set was produced by the American pharmaceutical company Ortho to promote birth-control pills and was distributed among doctors at a national conference for The American College of Obstetricians and Gynecologists. The box conflates drug packet design with the razzle-dazzle of magic, and contains a conventional range of children's magic tricks.

4. Clarks shumagic™/renovating polish, present day

This mass-produced product packaging features a photograph of the magician Robert Harbin (1909-79).

5. *Learn the Art of Magic*, Cleanliness Institute, New York, 1928

In this small pamphlet the public benefits of cleanliness are promoted metaphorically in a series of 'tricks'. We see how getting into the bathtub removes 'mysterious smudges' and how a towel dirty with handprints is a 'bad example of black magic'.

Magic Posters

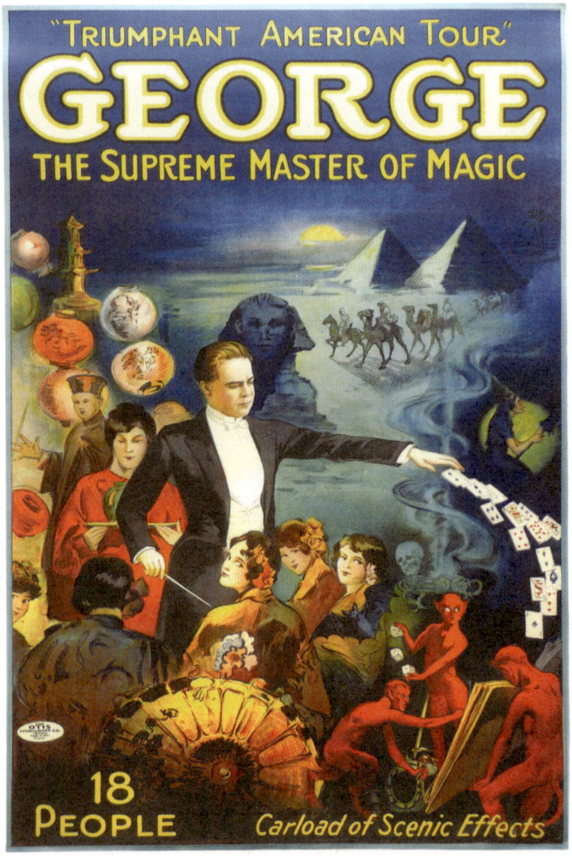

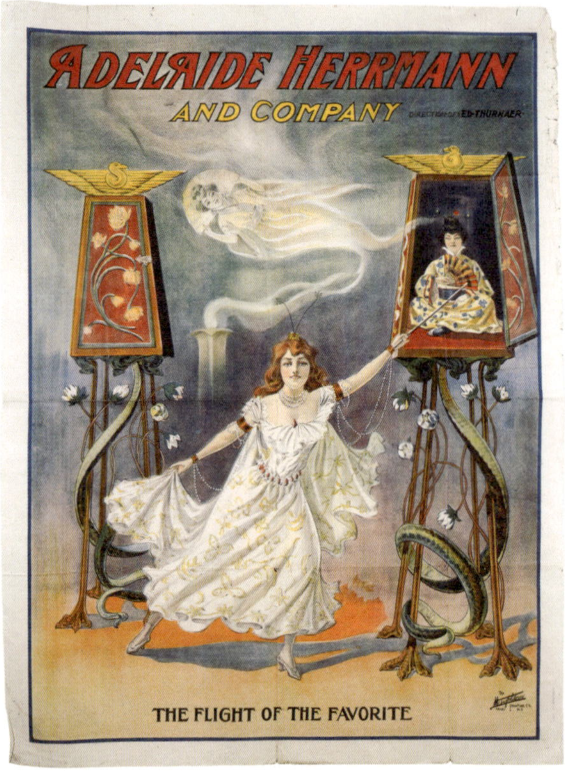

The history of magic is notoriously opaque, as it is in the magician's interest to exaggerate his or her powers and professional achievements and introduce hyperbole into publicity material. These posters reflect some of the key strategies repeatedly employed for impact on the public's imagination. They depict the magician as a princely commander of unearthly forces (fig. 1) or an empowered, ethereal female performer (fig. 2), which is very much in contrast to the more commonly sidelined assistant of recent eras. Outrageous claims that are both illogical and beguiling demonstrate how the habits of advertising carry across into this esoteric sector (fig.3). The final three posters (figs. 4–6) illustrate how the appropriation of non-Western identity was intended to embody exotic potentiality, the turban in turn connoting and obscuring, but always leading our expectations.

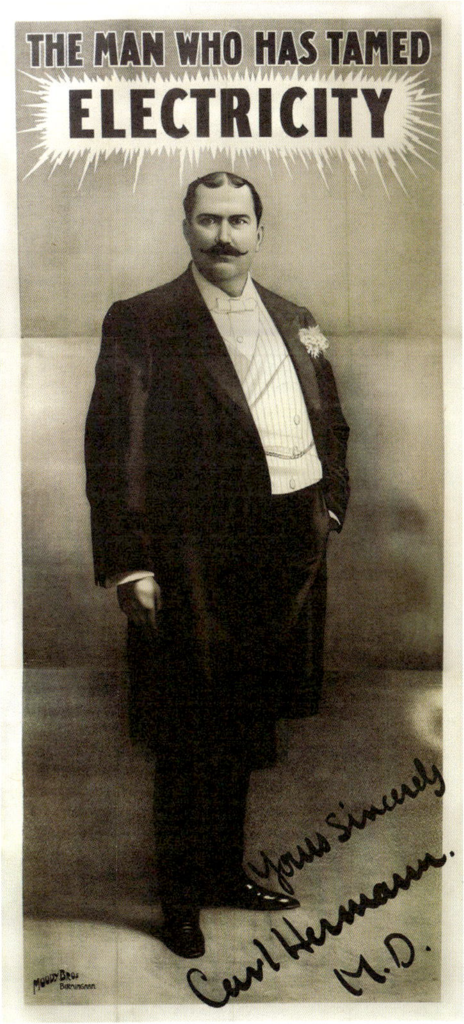
THE MAN WHO HAS TAMED
ELECTRICITY
Yours Sincerely
Carl Hermann
M.D.

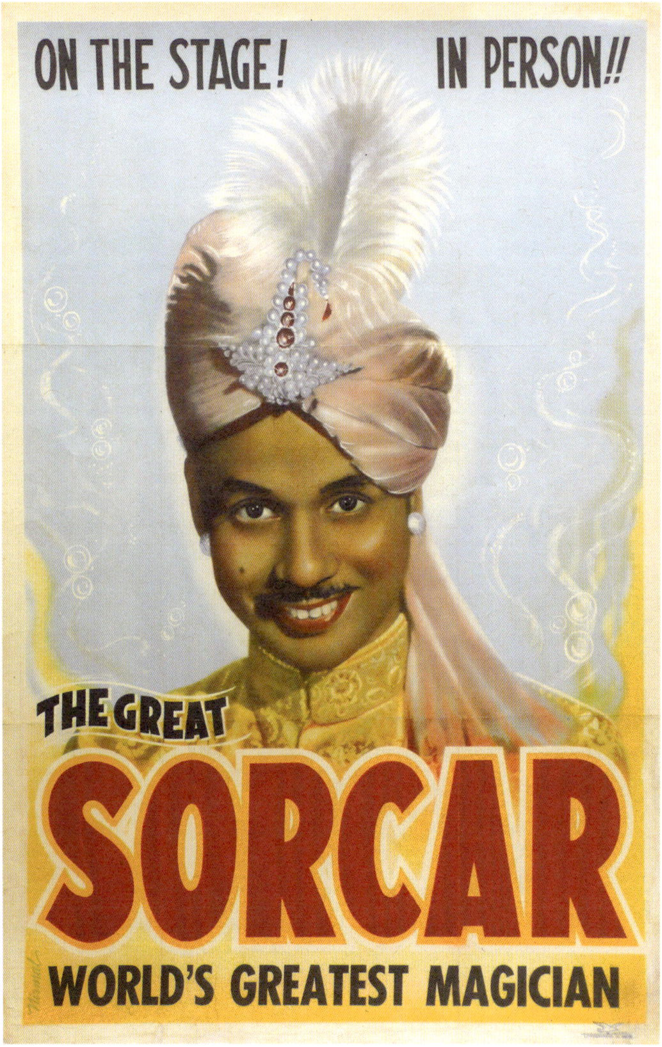
ON THE STAGE!
IN PERSON!!
THE GREAT
SORCAR
WORLD'S GREATEST MAGICIAN

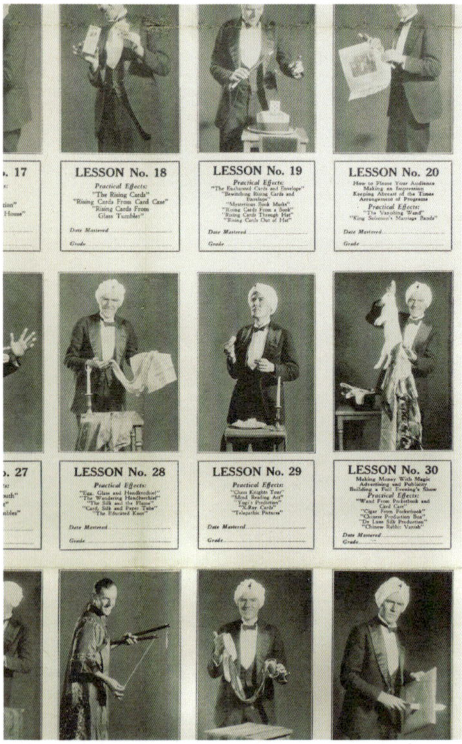
LESSON No. 18
Practical Effects:
"The Rising Cards"
"Rising Cards From Card Case"
"Rising Cards From Glass Tumbler"
Date Mastered
Grade
LESSON No. 19
Practical Effects:
"Mysterious Book Marks"
"Rising Cards From a Book"
"Rising Cards Through Hat"
"Rising Cards Out of Hat"
Date Mastered
Grade
LESSON No. 20
How to Please Your Audience
Making an Impression
Keeping Abreast of the Times
Arrangement of Programs
Practical Effects:
"The Vanishing Wand"
Date Mastered
Grade
LESSON No. 28
Practical Effects:
"The Silk and the Flame"
"Card, Silk and Paper Tube"
"The Educated Knot"
Date Mastered
Grade
LESSON No. 29
Practical Effects:
"Chess Knights Tour"
"Mind Reading Act"
"Yogi's Prediction"
"X-Ray Cards"
"Telepathic Pictures"
Date Mastered
Grade
LESSON No. 30
Making Money With Magic
Advertising and Publicity
Building a Full Evening's Show
Practical Effects:
"Wand From Pocketbook and Card Case"
"Cigar From Pocketbook"
"Chinese Production Box"
"De Luxe Silk Production"
"Chinese Rabbit Vanish"
Date Mastered
Grade

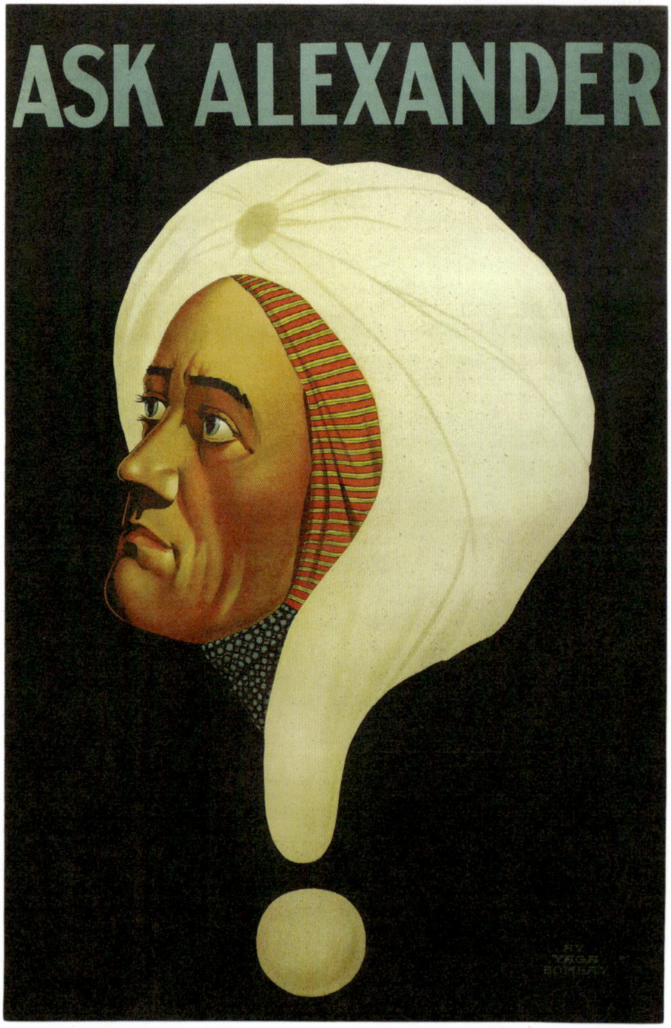
ASK ALEXANDER

1. *George: The Supreme Master of Magic*, 1924

George G. Grover (1887-1958) enjoyed considerable success in South and Central America. His North American tour, for which this poster was produced, was anything but 'Triumphant'. Attempting to follow in the footsteps of his much better known (and far wealthier) rival Howard Thurston, George secured a series of bookings in North American theatres and engaged Thurston's lithograph company to create spectacular posters for his appearances. Thurston, in an ungenerous act of professional sabotage, slapped injunctions on George's shows before he had the chance to appear in any significant theatre. Ironically, the failure of this tour, and the consequence that a relatively small number of the print run ever got pasted onto a wall, makes this one of the more commonly extant original stone lithographs. As a result, George's name has become much better known than it was during his lifetime.

2. *The Flight of the Favorite*, c.1901

Adelaide Herrmann (1853-1932) was born in London and was the widow of the illusionist Alexander Herrmann (1844-96), who had made his home in America. She took over her husband's show upon his death and, after three seasons with Alexander's nephew Leon Herrmann, performed independently for over 30 years. In 1918, at the age of 64, she opened her 'Temple of Magic' on Coney Island, and then continued touring America as 'The Queen of Magic' until her retirement due to ill-health in 1928. 'The Flight of the Favorite' illusion, featured during the early 1900s, featured the transposition of a girl from one raised cabinet to another on the opposite side of the stage.

3. *The Man Who Has Tamed Electricity*, c.1905

The unknown magician depicted here has taken his name, in all but a single 'r', from Carl (Compars) Herrmann (1816-87), brother-in-law of Adelaide Herrmann. Through an act in which he apparently tamed the powers of electricity, and by referring to himself as 'M.D.', he was copying another highly successful contemporary performer, Dr Walford Bodie MD, who had made his name (and his fortune) by claiming to be able to withstand a seemingly fatal level of electrical current, and later by setting up a bogus medical company selling tablets that conferred 'Bodic Force'. These spectacular acts exploited audiences' new fascination with the mysterious power, and methods often depended on the fact that few understood the difference between static and current electricity.

4. *The Great Sorcar*, c.1950

Padmashree Pratul Chandra Sarcar (1913-71) was the most successful Indian magician of his lifetime and toured extensively internationally. A world away from the comparatively brash aesthetics of his American rivals, this image depicts his gentle performing style. Sorcar created a sensation on British TV show 'Panorama', during a live transmission hosted by Richard Dimbleby in 1956, when a woman seemingly cut in half by a small circular saw failed to revive before the end of the show, causing the BBC switchboard to be jammed with complaints. Whether the timing was carefully planned as a publicity stunt is unknown, but the assistant lived to tell the tale. Sorcar's show was inherited by his son Prodip Chandra Sarcar, who is still performing as Sorcar Jnr.

5. *Tarbell Course of Magic*, instruction poster illustrating a mail order magic course, 1929 (detail)

The American magician Harlan Tarbell (1890-1960) wrote and illustrated 60 mail order magic lessons, published between 1926 and 1928. A mammoth project involving over 3,100 illustrations, The Tarbell Course of Magic is still in print as an eight-volume series. This poster was designed for students to display and tick off each chapter as the various magical skills were mastered.

6. *Ask Alexander*, c.1920

Claude Alexander Conlin (1880-1954), 'Alexander The Man Who Knows', was a phenomenally successful performer on the American Vaudeville circuit, specialising in mind-reading and spiritualistic effects. A somewhat colourful individual whose activities offstage seemingly included extortion, bigamy and possibly two murders, his most famous onstage effect involved answering audience questions sealed in envelopes out of his reach. One of his principal secrets was the 1920s equivalent of a bluetooth headset, which he concealed beneath the turban that became an integral part of his image.

L'Art Magique

An appendix of André Breton's book *L'Art Magique* (Paris: Club Français du Livre, 1957) reproduces responses from a number of key thinkers and practitioners to a series of questions posed on such issues as aesthetic pleasure, illusion, desire and enchantment. To follow is Breton's first question and a selection of responses.

André Breton
Some may have maintained recently (J.A. Rony, *La Magie*) that 'civilisation only dissipated the fiction of magic to glorify, through art, the magic of fiction'. Do you subscribe to this view? From the speculations of ancient magicians and modern artists on the possibilities and means of *enchanting the universe* – the magician apparently striving for the real, the artist the imaginary, whose short and long-term repercussions on the real are undeniable – would you conclude that their approach is driven by the same guiding principle and what, in your opinion, is the nature of that principle?

Maurice Blanchot
It seems to me that there is a paradox in all forms of magic that renders it attractive and superficial: it claims to be at once power, initiative and action, while in order to constitute itself it seeks to return to that point of universal indetermination that excludes every limit, every form, power, action. It wishes to act on the world, to manipulate it, but by means of that which is prior to the world, that 'on-this-side' where action is impossible.

Georges Bataille
Sociologists and ethnologists will not miss the opportunity to tell you that the magical character of a work of art signifies the desire of its authors to subordinate its material (poetic) value to practical efficacy... Confusion has arisen from the tendency to see in the work of art possible consequences for the real world beyond its most obvious effect, which acts upon the sensibility. It seems to me that this value, which is for you as for me the philosopher's stone in pursuit of which we live, can only be perceived without mystery, in pure material effect, allied only to those affective or active reactions that it elicits. Admittedly, in my view this effect is only accomplished by the negation of the real world.

Roger Caillois
Art and magic are complementary, and in consequence irreducible. There can only be incidental relationships between them. One must choose between the liberty of thought permitted and indeed assumed by aesthetic detachment, and the rigorous and immutable formalism implied by belief in magic. One may only appreciate a magical work aesthetically on the condition that one ceases to believe in the force it is held to transmit: without which, it is glaringly obvious that one is not first and foremost interested in its beauty but its liturgical power.

[...] As for magic, I note that the more an object is believed potent, the less need it has to be artistic: thus, in our time, the enamelled Saint Christophers that motorists attach to the dashboard of their cars, or the amulets sent, payment-on-receipt, by the magicians who recruit their clientele through small ads on the back pages of newspapers.

Perhaps the opposition is deeper still: Aladdin's lamp was not a beautiful lamp. Flying carpets are not renowned for the richness of their motifs or the harmony of their colours. In fairy tales, magical objects are objects like any other, more humble than any other. They have no special appearance. To the point that one may elicit a law, or at least a warning. Is it in order to let it be understood that he who imagines them to be art objects is condemned thereby always to pass by them without recognising them? After all, there would be some justice in that. Even one who does not believe in magic can derive from this incompatibility a lesson full of good sense.

Claude Lévi-Strauss

There are not only artists but also – still – magicians (bonesetters, seers, etc.) in contemporary society, who have little to do with art... Across history, and to varying extents in different societies, art and magic have doubtless sometimes travelled the same route, sometimes diverged, and sometimes crossed paths. Thus: there is something of the character of magic in Renaissance art, which is an attempt to appropriate the diversity and the materiality of the universe for the benefit of a bourgeoisie of owners; a motive that is perpetuated and inverted in modern painting – while the 'intellectuals' cannot possess real objects, they may at least make imaginary ones that will constitute their privilege. Then, with the gentrification of painting, another inversion, these imaginary objects are 'worth' as much as real ones. In a sense then, art is certainly magic, but in outlining the relation, I perceive at once the difference: magic seeks to obtain 'real' effects (an abundant harvest, the love of a woman, the death of an enemy) without ever succeeding, whereas art succeeds in its enterprise, but always as travesty or in imaginary forms.

Leonora Carrington

Return to the source of things.

Until the artist has become once more a magician, that is, until he masters magical art, beginning with himself, one can but say that ends in art are as dangerous and confused as weapons in the hands of politicians and heads of state. Fortunately, mankind is generally much too insensitive to feel the influences spat out by its brother artists. Ignorance, too, offers protection. The man who resembles a piece of meat, who is more or less dead, has nothing to fear. The 'sensitive' man suffers for it, without knowing why, and sometimes dies of it. Then let us explore the possibility that we may have subtle instruments that will permit us to radiate or to receive a benevolent magic, while cultivating defences against the multiple poisons of the invisible world. Only in the strange magical ocean can we find salvation for ourselves and our sick planet.

François le Lionnais

I am convinced that the decline of belief in magic and occultism would constitute favourable conditions for a truly magical art to flourish, an art of a more troubling imagination, a greater liberty. It is in turning our backs on magic and occultism – in which I see only mediocre, dusty idols deprived of all potency – and in interrogating our sensual emotions, our affective passions, the renovation of intellectual structures imposed by scientific progress, that we will liberate our imagination from the restrictions that paralyse it and awaken to a life and art that are magical.

[...] As I do not believe that magic can attain any of the aims that it seeks, I can scarcely accord it any chance of rehabilitation, at least in principal. It is towards life (actions, sensations, feelings), towards art, towards science that we should turn to try and find that which we wish, in error, to find in occultism. If however – as a result of some improbable yet not impossible aberration in civilisation – magic were to be rehabilitated, I should regret it. Indeed, I am convinced that such a resurgence would entail in art a regression towards banality and sclerosis; the most gifted would only come to terms with it at the price of an attenuation of their freshness and their creative originality; others would not survive.

List of Exhibited Works

Measurements are given in centimetres, height before width and depth. Photographs have been supplied by the artists or their representatives and works are © the artist or the estate of the artist, unless otherwise stated.

Jonathan Allen
Kalanag Double, 2009 (p. 45)
Pigment print
50 x 65
Courtesy the artist
Props courtesy the John Fisher Collection
Photograph: Mark Enstone

Archive (Chris Kubick & Anne Walsh)
Yves Klein Speaks!, 2002
Audio CD
65 minutes, 10 seconds
Courtesy the artist

Zoe Beloff
A Modern Case of Possession, 2007 (p. 49)
History of a Fixed Idea, 2007
3D video installations, various media
Dimensions variable
Courtesy the artist
Musical Director: Shelley Hirsch
Technical Realisation: Eric Muzzy

Ansuman Biswas & Jem Finer
Zero Genie, 2001 (p. 51)
DVD video projection
Courtesy the artist

Joan Brossa
Eina morta, 1988
Wood, metal, scissors
7.5 x 23 x 23
Courtesy Fundació Joan Brossa
© Fundació Joan Brossa and DACS, London, 2009

Sense atzar, 1988 (p. 53)
Wood, playing cards, padlock
12 x 25 x 25
Courtesy Fundació Joan Brossa
Photograph: Jordi Tost
© Fundació Joan Brossa and DACS, London, 2009

Portant, 1989
Wood, pen stand and magic wands
22 x 36.5 x 22.5
Courtesy Fundació Joan Brossa
© Fundació Joan Brossa and DACS, London, 2009

Rick Buckley
From the series *The Incomplete Man*
Courtesy the artist

Cult #1, 2008 (p. 55)
Laser photocopy
34 x 25.5

Smoke, 2008
Laser photocopy
27 x 19

Lost & Found, 1994
Black-and-white Polaroid photographs
10.7 x 8.5 and 9 x 8.2

Entrance, 2008
Laser photocopy
32.5 x 22

King's Crown, 2009
Piezo pigment print
51 x 68.5

Mask # 1, 2008
Piezo pigment print
67 x 50

Globe of Fire, 2007
Graphite on paper
83 x 62

Rhombicuboctahedron, 2007
Graphite on paper
47 x 48

Funfair, 2008
Laser photocopy
30 x 40

Gate, 2008
Laser photocopy
31.5 x 40

In out / out In, 2005
Ink on paper
72 x 52

Vapour, 2007
China white pencil on paper
70 x 50

The Incomplete Man, 2009 (text extracts)
Five offset prints on acid-free rag paper
48 x 32 each

Brian Catling
Notes & Bones from a Conjuror's Table, 2009 (p. 57)
Mixed media
200 x 200
Courtesy the artist

Center for Tactical Magic
The Ultimate Jacket (Prototype #5), 2004
Mixed media (wearable garment with fifty concealed pockets)
Dimensions variable
Courtesy the artist

Jackie & Denise Chapwoman
When Art Critics Go Bad (Arachnokitty), 2001/2006 (p. 61)
Oil on canvas
48.3 x 63.5
Courtesy the artist and White Cube, London
Photograph: Todd-White Art Photography

Tom Friedman
Untitled (A Curse), an eleven-inch spherical space eleven inches above a pedestal cursed by a witch, 1992 (p. 63)
Spherical space, pedestal
132 x 28 x 28
Private Collection of Harry Handelsman
Courtesy Gagosian Gallery, London

Brian Griffiths
Daylight Ned, 2007 (p. 65)
Wood (various), paint, wood stain, varnish, brogue shoes
131 x 71 x 50
Courtesy the artist and Vilma Gold, London
Photograph: Andy Keate

The Only Living, 2007
Canvas, acrylic paint, eyelets, rope and fixings
350 x 250
Courtesy the artist and Vilma Gold, London

The Only Living, 2007
Canvas, acrylic paint, eyelets, rope and fixings
350 x 250
Courtesy the artist and Vilma Gold, London

Colin Guillemet
Untitled (anything but a rabbit), 2006 (p. 67)
11 pairs of SX-70 Polaroid photographs
10.7 x 17.6 each
Courtesy the artist

João Maria Gusmão & Pedro Paiva
Paramagnetism, 2004 (p. 69)
16mm film projection
1 minute, 33 seconds
Courtesy the artists

Cinematic (or the log enchanter), 2006
16mm film projection
1 minute, 50 seconds
Courtesy the artists

The Rolling Stones, 2007
16mm film projection
2 minutes, 3 seconds
Courtesy the artists

Film on a Skeleton, 2004/6
16mm film projection
30 seconds
Courtesy the artists

The Myth of the Spirit of Gravity - part 2, 2007
16mm film projection
3 minutes, 42 seconds
Courtesy the artists

Susan Hiller
Homage to Yves Klein, 2008 (p. 71)
150 black-and-white digital photographs
170 x 170
Courtesy Timothy Taylor Gallery, London

Alexandra Hopf
Gehülfe D (Assistant D), 2007 (p. 73)
Gehülfe P (Assistant P), 2007
Gehülfe R (Assistant R), 2007
Gehülfe S (Assistant S), 2007
Spray paint on glass mounted on hessian board
54 x 47 x 4 each
Courtesy the artist

Christian Jankowski
Telemistica, 1999 (p. 75)
DVD video with sound
22 minutes
Courtesy the artist and Lisson Gallery, London

Janice Kerbel
Home Conjuring Unit, 2000 (p. 77)
Double-sided digital inkjet print
59.4 x 84
Courtesy the artist and Greengrassi, London

Annika Lundgren
Magic & Politics, 2007 (p. 79)
DVD digital slideshow projection
13 minutes, 10 seconds
Courtesy the artist

Juan Muñoz
Untitled, 1995 (p. 81)
3 pairs of black-and-white photographs
12 x 12 each
Courtesy The Estate of Juan Muñoz

Untitled, 1995
Black-and-white photographs, ink
71 x 51
Courtesy The Estate of Juan Muñoz

Bruce Nauman
Failing to Levitate in the Studio, 1966 (p. 83)
Black-and-white photograph mounted on masonite
50.8 x 61
Courtesy the artist
Photo courtesy Sperone Westwater, New York
© ARS, New York, and DACS, London, 2009

Ian Saville
Performance of Socialist Magic at *Magic Show* tour venues 2009/10
Duration variable

Ariel Schlesinger
Netally and I, 2006 (p. 87)
Painted wood, aluminum, rubber
0.7 x 15 x 3
Courtesy Galerija Gregor Podnar Berlin / Ljubljana

L'angoisse de la page blanche, 2008
A4 paper, wood, electric motor
65 x 55 x 20
Courtesy the artist and Dvir Gallery, Tel Aviv

Suzanne Treister
ALCHEMY/Al-Ahram, 31st January - 6th February 2008, 2008 (p. 89)
ALCHEMY/The Financial Times, 28th June 2007, 2007
ALCHEMY/Jüdische Allgemeine, 10th April 2008, 2008
Watercolour and felt-tip pen on watercolour paper
152.5 x 122 each
Courtesy Annely Juda Fine Art, London

Sinta Werner
Site-specific installation at QUAD, Derby and The Grundy Gallery, Blackpool, 2009/2010
Dimensions variable
Courtesy the artist

Conjuring Consent

A selection of the following items will appear in the Conjuring Consent archive at *Magic Show* tour venues. Items marked * were photographed for this book by Tim Marshall, † by Joanna Fernandes, Tate Photography and ** by Jonathan Allen.

Adelaide Herrmann and company/The Flight of the Favorite, c.1901 (p. 104)
Unknown poster artist
Stone lithograph poster
104 x 77.5
Edwin A. Dawes Collection
© Edwin A. Dawes Collection

The Art of Illusion, 1945* (p. 99)
Booklet
19.5 x 14
Jonathan Allen Collection

Ask Alexander, c.1920** (p. 106)
Unknown poster artist
Stone lithograph poster mounted on linen
105 x 69.5
Paul Kieve Collection

Bang Gun, 1950s* (p. 93)
Aluminium prop
26 x 21
The Magic Circle Museum, London

Harry M. Bromley/Christian Magician, 1947* (p. 101)
Black-and-white photograph
19 x 25
Jonathan Allen Collection

Derren Brown's *Trick or Treat* featuring Jake and Dinos Chapman and Adrian Searle
Series one, episode two
Excerpt (8 minutes, 12 seconds), outtake (1 minute, 39 seconds)
First broadcast 20 April 2007
Courtesy Channel Four and Objective Productions
© Objective Productions

Card cross, 1992* (p. 100)
Playing cards
36 x 26 x 6
Courtesy Dan Wolfe
© Dan Wolfe 2009

Card-Finding Duck, c.1980* (p. 94)
Wooden prop with moving mechanical parts, deck of playing cards
25 x 31 x 11
Scott Penrose Collection

Clarks shumagic™/renovating polish, c.1990s* (p. 103)
Plastic tube, polish
12 x 5 x 3
Lionel Russell Collection

Conradi-Horster magic catalogue, 1932-33
Trade publication
23 x 15
Peter Lane Collection
© Peter Lane Collection

Mr Core's Balancing Tricks, 1940
Booklet
16.5 x 8.5
Private Collection

'Dead or Alive' trick, c.1940* (p. 99)
6 x printed paper portraits 10 x 10 each
1 x instruction sheet 21.5 x 14.5
John Fisher Collection

Demon Telegraph magic catalogues, c.1940s
Trade publications
21.5 x 14
Davenports Magic Company, London

Dock Haley Gospel Magic Company 'Life Insurance Policy' trick, c.2000
Printed paper trick
10.5 x 24
Jonathan Allen Collection

Documentary photographs of Fidel Castro at a rally in Cuba, January 1959
AP/Wide World
Dimensions variable

Documentary photographs of the magician Kalanag performing to Adolf Hitler, c.1936
Two reprinted black-and-white photographs
Dimensions variable
Unknown photographer

Dulux™ paint samples
Illusion, Illusionist, Invisible Green, Magic Carpet, Magic Cream, Thai Magic

The 'Electro' victory stand, c.1940* (p. 98)
Davenports Magic Company
Metal, lightbulbs, batteries
22 x 22.5 x 10.5
The Magic Circle Museum, London

'Fair Deal' trick, c.1970* (p. 96)
10 silkscreened cards, instruction sheet
12 x 18 each card
International Magic Collection, London

'Find Ugly' trick, 1997* (p. 101)
Jumbo playing cards
11.5 x 17.5
Courtesy Dan Wolfe
© Dan Wolfe 2009

Gallaher's Cigarette Cards, 1933 (p. 10)
Tricks and Puzzles series
6.5 x 3.5 each
Jonathan Allen Collection

Gasbag to Gasmask 1, c.1940* (p. 99)
Reversible prop
Cloth, papier-mâché, metal
30 x 21 x 21
Peter Lane Collection
© Peter Lane Collection

Gasbag to Gasmask 2, c.1940* (p. 99)
Reversible prop
Cloth, papier-mâché, metal
30 x 21 x 21
Derrick Speight Collection

Genii / The Conjurors' Magazine, 1960† (p. 102)
Volume 25, No.2, October 1960
27 x 20
Tim Reed Collection
© The Genii Corporation. All Rights Reserved

George the Supreme Master of Magic, 1924** (p. 104)
Unknown poster artist
Stone lithograph poster mounted on linen
105 x 69.5
Paul Kieve Collection

The Great Sorcar/World's Greatest Magician, c.1950** (p. 105)
Unknown poster artist
Lithograph poster mounted on linen
76 x 50.5
Paul Kieve Collection

Japanese cups and balls, late nineteenth century* (p. 95)
Toleware, cork
8 x 7.5 (each)
The Magic Circle Museum, London

Kalanag Revue, c.1959
Magic show programme
21 x 15
John Fisher Collection

Learn the Art of Magic, 1928* (p. 103)
Booklet
9.5 x 7.5
Private Collection

Magician's gimmicks, c.1970s-90s* (p. 95)
Dimensions and materials variable
Scott Penrose Collection

The Magic of Ortho, 1990* (p. 103)
Magic set
7.6 x 33 x 53
Private Collection

Magic with a Message, 1956
Spiral bound booklet
By David Hoy, illustrated by Sid Couchey
Published by Revell, Westwood, New Jersey
17 x 23
Jonathan Allen Collection

The Man Who Has Tamed Electricity/Carl Hermann MD, c.1905** (p. 105)
Unknown poster artist
Stone lithograph poster mounted on linen
221 x 102.5
Paul Kieve Collection
© Paul Kieve Collection

The Movie Fan, 1940
Weekly periodical
31 x 24
Jonathan Allen Collection

The Oxo Book of Magic, 1934* (p. 102)
Booklet
Published by Oxo Ltd, London
19 x 12
Private Collection

Pears Soap adverts, c.1900
Advertising flyers
22 x 14.5
John Fisher Collection

RAF paper tearing trick, c.1940
Printed envelope, folded tissue paper
28 x 10
The Magic Circle Museum, London

Ian Saville cabaret performances, 2006-9
Video documentation exhibited at selected *Magic Show* venues
Duration variable
Courtesy the artist

Ian Saville's Karl Marx ventriloquist prop (first version), c.1980
Colour print on modified hardboard
52 x 41
Courtesy the artist

Seeing Truth: Object Lessons with Magical and Mechanical Devices, 1910* (p. 101)
By C H Woolston
20 x 14
Jonathan Allen Collection

Stanley Collins' scrapbook of magic cartoons, c.1883-1950s† (p. 97)
37 x 26 x 7.5
Edwin A. Dawes Collection
© Edwin A. Dawes Collection

Tarbell Course of Magic, 1929** (p. 106)
Unknown poster artist
Offset print mounted on linen
90 x 59.5
Paul Kieve Collection

'Wand through card' trick, c.1960* (p. 95)
Magic wand, playing card
Length 34
The Magic Circle Museum, London

List of Illustrations

The following illustrations are listed in the order in which they appear in this book. Photographs of artworks have been supplied by the artists or their representatives and works are © the artist or the estate of the artist, unless otherwise stated.

Hieronymus Bosch (c.1450-1516)
The Conjurer (p. 16)
Oil on panel, pre-restoration
Musée d'Art et d'Histoire, Saint-Germain-en-Laye, France/Giraudon/The Bridgeman Art Library

Marcel Duchamp
Bicycle Wheel (1951 after lost original of 1913) (p. 27)
Metal wheel, painted wooden stool
128.3 x 63.8 x 42
The Sidney and Harriet Janis Collection, Museum of Modern Art, New York; courtesy The Museum of Modern Art, New York/Scala, Florence
© Succession Marcel Duchamp/ADAGP, Paris and DACS, London 2009

Broadside advertising a performance by Caroline Bernhardt, 1846 (p. 29)
Courtesy Collection of Christina and Volker Huber, Offenbach

Photograph from Howard Thurston's 'Workbooks', c.1910–11 (p. 31)
Courtesy Mike Caveney, Egyptian Hall Museum

Shell game, as used by Fred Kaps, c.1975 (p. 33)
Walnut shells, sponge balls, spectacles case
6 x 15 x 8
Courtesy The Magic Circle Museum, London

Documentary photograph of Jay Ose and Man Ray at the Magic Castle, Hollywood (p. 35)
First published in *Genii*, Volume 31, No.5, January 1967 pp.221-222
© The Genii Corporation
All Rights Reserved

Fattura della morte, c.1891 (p. 37)
Accession number 1892.64.1
Collection of the Pitt Rivers Museum
Courtesy Pitt Rivers Museum, University of Oxford

Jonathan Allen
Tommy Angel #1, 2005 (p. 44)
Pigment print
122 x 91
Photograph: Mark Enstone

Zoe Beloff
A restored model of Albert Grass's proposed Dreamland amusement park, 2009 (p. 48)
Mixed media
190 x 190
Photograph: Brad Paris

Ansuman Biswas & Jem Finer
wave/particle, 2001 (p. 50) (detail)
Video still

Joan Brossa
Poema visual, 1982 (p. 52)
Screenprint
50 x 35
Courtesy Fundació Joan Brossa
© Fundació Joan Brossa and DACS, London, 2009

Rick Buckley
Monument, 2008 (p. 54)
Mirror, wood
164 x 54 x 54

Brian Catling
Madremanya Magi, 2009 (p. 56)
Digital photograph
Courtesy the artist and Denys Blacker

Center for Tactical Magic
Psychic Surveillance, 2009 (p. 58)
Digital print on vinyl
244 x 325

Television still from Derren Brown's *Trick or Treat*,
Series one, episode two (p. 60)
© Objective Productions

Tom Friedman
Untitled (Dollar Print), 2000 (p. 62)
36 one-dollar bills
35.5 x 89.5
Courtesy Gagosian Gallery, New York

Brian Griffiths
Traitor, 2008 (p. 64)
Brass horn, plastic, varnish
85 x 20 x 24
Courtesy the artist and Vilma Gold, London
Photograph: Andy Keate

Colin Guillemet
Canary Shift, 2005 (p. 66)
Live canary, canthaxanthine, cage, table
Dimensions variable

João Maria Gusmão & Pedro Paiva
About the spirit of gravity (or the blacksmith and the cutting of the serpent) 2nd version, 2007 (p. 68)
16mm film, colour, no sound
2 minutes, 42 seconds
Commissioned by Zé dos Bois (ZDB), Lisbon and filmed in Morocco

Alexandra Hopf
The Destiny Maschine, 2009 (p. 72)
Installation view at Sox, Berlin
Spraypaint on glass
Dimensions variable
Photograph: Anne Neukamp

Christian Jankowski
The Holy Artwork, 2001 (p. 74)
DVD still
Television broadcast, performance and colour DVD
Courtesy the artist and Lisson Gallery, London

Janice Kerbel
Three Marked Decks: Bicycle Riderback (poker), 1999 (detail) (p. 76)
Three Marked Decks: Bee Special Diamondback (blackjack), 1999 (detail) (p. 76)
Offset lithographs
60 x 100 each
Courtesy the artist and Greengrassi, London

Annika Lundgren
Levitating Hat Trick, 2009 (p. 78)
Black-and-white photographs
33 x 22

Juan Muñoz
The Wasteland, 1987 (p. 80)
Collection of Elayne and Marvin Mordes, USA
Photograph © Tate Photography
© The Estate of Juan Muñoz

Bruce Nauman
Falls, Pratfalls and Sleights of Hand (Clean Version), 1993 (p. 82)
Video still
Collection of Kunstmuseum Wolfsburg
Courtesy Kunstmuseum Wolfsburg
© ARS, NY and DACS, London 2009

Ian Saville
Karl Marx ventriloquist prop (second version), c.1980 (p. 85)
Colour print on modified hardboard
87 x 61
Photographs: Jonathan Allen

Ariel Schlesinger
Bubble Machine, 2006 (p. 86)
Wood, electric drill, ladder, soap, cooking gas, grill, transformer, stool, glass
230 x 200 x 210
Courtesy the artist and Dvir Gallery, Tel Aviv

Suzanne Treister
GEMATRIA/40 Jewish Magicians, 2009 (detail) (p. 88)
Inkjet, water and Rotring pen on paper
62 x 112
Courtesy Annely Juda Fine Art, London

Sinta Werner
Disjunction, 2007 (p. 90)
Installation view at Goldsmiths MFA show 2007
MDF, chipboard, paint
370 x 350 x 400

Notes on Contributors

Jonathan Allen is a visual artist whose work has featured in many solo and group exhibitions since the early 1990s. In 2007 he guest-edited an issue of the New York-based art and culture quarterly *Cabinet*, and was the Arts Council England Helen Chadwick Fellow 2007–8 at the University of Oxford and the British School at Rome. He is a consultant curator at The Magic Circle Museum, London.

Sally O'Reilly is a regular contributor to many art and culture publications, and has written essays on emerging and established artists for international galleries and institutions, as well as the book *The Body in Contemporary Art* (Thames & Hudson, 2009). She was co-editor of the thematic, interdisciplinary broadsheet *Implicasphere* (2003–8) and is a dean of Brown Mountain College of the Performing Arts, an itinerant platform for the production of performative events.

Simon During is Professor of English at Johns Hopkins University and the author of *Modern Enchantments*, Harvard, 2002.

Brigitte Felderer is a writer and independent curator and teaches at the University of Applied Arts Vienna. She devised and curated *Zauberkünste* for the Nordico-Museum der Stadt Linz, Austria, 2009.

Peter Lamont is a historian and psychologist who teaches at the University of Edinburgh. He has published extensively on the history and psychology of magic.

Pierre Taillefer studied political science and art history in France, Chile and Germany. He is currently working on a history of magic from Antiquity to the Renaissance.

Helen Varola is a New York-based independent curator who, with her husband and magic historian P.G. Varola, co-curated *Con Art* at Site Gallery, Sheffield, 2002.

Marina Warner is a writer and Professor of Literature, Film and Theatre Studies at the University of Essex. She was curatorial advisor for *Eyes, Lies and Illusions* at the Hayward Gallery, 2004.